The Ideal Client Map:

The Entrepreneur's Guide to Creating a Clear Branding Strategy and Actionable Marketing Plan So You Can Reach More Qualified Leads

MONTE ARMSTRONG & ANZA GOODBAR

Copyright & Disclaimer

http://mapyouridealclient.com

Published by TechStrong Marketing

Limits of Liability / Disclaimer of Warranty

The author and publisher of this book and the accompanying materials have used their best efforts in preparing this program. The author and publisher make no representation or warranties with respect to the accuracy, applicability, fitness, or completeness of the contents of this material. They disclaim any warranties (expressed or implied), merchantability, or fitness for any particular purpose. The author and publisher shall in no event be held liable for any loss or other damages, including but not limited to special, incidental, consequential, or other damages.

The author does not guarantee specific results from implementing the advice and strategies presented in this book. Individual results may vary, and success depends on a variety of factors, including but not limited to personal effort, market conditions, and unforeseen events. The information provided in this book is for educational purposes only and should not be considered legal or professional advice.

The author and publisher do not warrant the performance, effectiveness, or applicability of any sites listed in this book. All links are for information purposes only and are not warranted for content, accuracy, or any other implied or explicit purpose.

Dear Readers,
As you embark on this fantastic journey through our co-authored book, you'll come across various links sprinkled throughout the pages. These links may whisk you away to fascinating products, valuable services, enticing offers, and yes, affiliate opportunities. You might also stumble upon exclusive membership offers designed to enhance your experience. We want to be transparent with you: clicking on these links and making purchases might just result in us earning a little something – potentially even making money. But rest assured, any compensation we receive goes towards fueling our passion for creating more valuable and enriching content for you!

It's important to know that you could indeed obtain any affiliate offer directly from the source for the exact same price. That said, when you choose to engage through our links, you get access to unique bonuses that we've meticulously curated with your best interests at heart. You're not saving money by bypassing us, but you might miss out on these special extras that come at no additional cost to you. We see it as a win-win: you get more value, and we get to keep doing what we love.

Here's a little secret – when you decide to click, buy, try, or sign up for anything additional through this book or our membership area, you're directly supporting us. And for that, we thank you profusely. Your support not only motivates us but also enables us to create even more tailored resources and engaging content to meet your needs. Consider it a small yet impactful way to keep the wheels of this awesome journey spinning.

So go ahead, explore the possibilities our links offer. Whether it's that perfect product, service, or irresistible offer you've been dreaming of, we hope you find exactly what you're looking for. And just know, every click means you're not just enhancing your own experience, but also helping us continue to bring you high-quality content. Thank you from the bottom of our hearts for your unwavering support.

Best,
Monte Armstrong and Anza Goodbar

PS- Everyone's results will vary. What, where, who to, when, why, and how you sell things will drastically affect your results.

Without any plan at all, your results will stink regardless.

Dedications

Monte's Dedications:

Steven Lai – The original inspiration behind the entire mapping idea.

Carl Alleyne – Carl introduced me to mind mapping in the first place. THANKS!

Anza Goodbar – Before we ever talked about co-authoring, you provided feedback and validation which motivated me to evolve TICM into more. Thank You! For that initial support and for joining me on this collaborative journey.

The Members of Copy And Content Secrets – Thank You for all your support, feedback, and contributions to TICM and all the goodies that go with it.

Special Thanks to Jim Edwards (and team) – Without you all, I would not have been able to travel so far and so quickly in my entrepreneurial journey.

Anza's Dedications:

I want to express my gratitude to Monte Armstrong for involving me in this incredible project. His insights and The Ideal Client tool have transformed my approach to creating accurate client avatars. I'm truly inspired by Monte's expertise and look forward to applying his strategies to enhance my business. Working with him has been a transformative experience, and I'm excited to see the impact this collaboration will have.

I'm incredibly grateful to Jim Edwards for sharing his wisdom and insights in his book Copywriting Secrets. The Jim Edward's method to writing has completely revolutionized my business and approach to marketing. Using his tools CopyandContent.ai, I've been able to streamline my marketing approach and provide higher quality content to a larger audience than I could have ever imagined doing on my own.

I am truly grateful for the invaluable entrepreneurial experience that I have gained from my family. As a child, I had the opportunity to learn and glean expertise from my parents, which provided me with a significant head start on my own entrepreneurial journey. Their guidance not only instilled essential business acumen in me but also helped shape my outlook on life and work ethics. I cherish the lessons learned and the wisdom imparted by my family, as they have been instrumental in shaping my entrepreneurial path and contributing to my personal and professional growth.

Table of Contents

Introduction

Hello, entrepreneurs and small business owners! Congratulations on taking the first step towards reaching more qualified leads and making a bigger impact with your business. You've just purchased "The Ideal Client Map: The Entrepreneur's Guide to Creating a Clear Branding Strategy and Actionable Marketing Plan So You Can Reach More Qualified Leads" and we're here to tell you that you've made a great decision.

As the authors, Monte Armstrong and Anza Goodbar, we have a combined total of 40+ years of expertise in copywriting, sales, and defining ideal client avatars. We're here to guide you through the process of creating a clear branding strategy and actionable marketing plan.

We know how daunting it can be to navigate the world of marketing and business development on your own. That's why we've written this book to provide you with practical advice, tips, tricks, and real-life examples to help you master this important topic.

"The Ideal Client Map" isn't just another marketing book filled with generic advice. We've included the mistakes to avoid, and we're going to help you define your ideal customer's emotional hot buttons better than ever before. By the time you finish this book, you'll have a clear understanding of who your ideal client is and how to effectively reach them.

So, what are you waiting for? The book you purchased is right in your hands. It's time to dive in and start learning how to create a clear branding strategy and actionable marketing plan that will help you reach more qualified leads and make a bigger impact with your business.

We're confident that "The Ideal Client Map" will provide you with the guidance you need to take your business to the next level. Let's get started and make the most out of the book you've already invested in.

Author's Bio

Monte Armstrong, a seasoned business professional with over 25 years of successful sales experience, has partnered with Anza Goodbar, an established serial entrepreneur and business consultant with over 15 years of copywriting expertise.

Together, they have co-authored "The Ideal Client Map: The Entrepreneur's Guide to Creating a Clear Branding Strategy and Actionable Marketing Plan So You Can Reach More Qualified Leads." This comprehensive guide is designed to help entrepreneurs and small business owners define their ideal client and connect with more qualified leads in a confident and strategic manner.

Monte's extensive sales background, combined with his role as a technology coach and creator of The Ideal Client Map online training, uniquely qualifies him to guide entrepreneurs towards their goals. Having started a successful local small business from scratch, he knows firsthand the struggles that come with running a business. His personal journey of transforming an emerging business into a thriving source of income serves as the foundation for the actionable strategies outlined in the book. With his expert insights and track record of success, he is the ideal mentor for those seeking to define their ideal client and attract more qualified leads.

Anza, on the other hand, brings over 15 years of copywriting experience and a deep understanding of the transformative power of content marketing to the table. As the Founder and CEO of Influence HER Digital Marketing Solutions, she is passionate about helping entrepreneurs and small business owners navigate the complexities of business development. Through "The Ideal Client Map," she aims to provide a comprehensive guide for creating a strong branding strategy and actionable marketing plan that will elevate businesses to new heights and help them stand out in a competitive market.

The combined expertise of Monte and Anza offers entrepreneurs the opportunity to take charge of their marketing strategy and start reaching the clients they truly deserve. If you are tired of spending endless hours on tasks that don't align with your passions, "The Ideal Client Map" is the solution you've been looking for. It's time to connect with your ideal clients and catapult your business to success.

"The Blanket Approach"

Assuming Everyone is in Your Target Audience Spells Disaster

Not Identifying an Ideal Audience is a Big Mistake.
For many entrepreneurs and small business owners, one of the biggest mistakes they can make in business development is assuming that everyone is their client. This is essentially the same as not giving it any thought at all, and it can spell disaster for a business in the long run.

How does including everyone in your target audience spell disaster?
First and foremost, not identifying a specific target audience means your marketing and business development efforts will be scattered and unfocused. This can lead to wasted time and resources, as you try to appeal to a broad range of individuals who may not actually be interested in your products or services.

Even worse, you may attract the wrong individuals entirely. Appealing to everyone leads to a ton of special requests, annoying questions, and completely unscalable projects. This just creates extra work and frustration as you spend more time catering to everyone instead of efficiently completing profitable jobs.

Additionally, assuming that everyone is your client means that you're not taking the time to truly understand the needs and pain points of a specific group of people. This lack of understanding can result in products or services that don't resonate with anyone in particular, leading to lackluster sales and lack of customer loyalty.

Finally, not identifying a target audience can also make it incredibly difficult to effectively position your brand in the marketplace. Without a clear understanding of who your ideal audience is, you'll struggle to create messaging and branding that truly speaks to their needs and desires.

Why is this assumption so commonplace?

1. **Lack of Confidence:** Entrepreneurs may fear they will be missing out on potential customers if they narrow their focus too much, so they cast a wide net in the hopes of catching as many clients as possible.

2. **Lack of Understanding:** Some entrepreneurs may believe that their own products and services are universally appealing, or everyone will make their own personal connection, and thus fail to see the need for targeting a specific audience.

3. **Assumption:** The old school brick and mortar retail store model has drilled the concept into our societal minds that you need to serve everyone. Many business owners may feel that they need to attract as many customers as possible in order to succeed,

leading them to take a blanket approach to their marketing and business development efforts.

Entrepreneurs and business owners are most likely to make the mistake of assuming everyone is their ideal client in the early stages of their business, when they're still trying to figure out who their target audience is and what their unique value proposition is. However, this mistake can also occur at later stages, particularly when a business is looking to expand and attract new customers.

Consequences:
Making the mistake that you must cater to everyone on the plant can have dire consequences for entrepreneurs and small business owners when they are developing a business. By not identifying a target audience at all, you risk wasting time, resources, and money trying to market to a broad, undefined group of people.

These consequences are MUCH worse than you think because without a specific target audience, your marketing efforts will lack focus and direction. You'll struggle to craft a message that resonates with anyone, leading to poor engagement and low conversion rates. This lack of clarity can also hinder product development and customer service, as you won't have a clear understanding of your customers' needs and preferences.

Let Me Tell You a Story About Discovering I Actually Hated My Business

"I am Monte, and I took a leap of faith by starting my own computer repair and IT support business solely based on my passion and technical expertise. I had no business background, no family members or friends who owned their own business, and no education in business. But I was determined to make it work.

I worked tirelessly, soliciting every business I could, taking on every job that came my way, and I was successful at increasing profits every year. My business built a strong local brand reputation, and I received consistent word-of-mouth referrals. I was living my dream, or so I thought.

What I didn't admit, not even to myself, was that I was working 70+ hours a week, seven days a week. I dreaded every time the phone rang because it meant more work piling up. I couldn't enjoy any time off because of the overwhelming workload waiting for me when I returned to my office. So, I found myself not taking any time off at all. I didn't want to hire anyone to help me because that would increase overhead, paperwork, and add another level of complexity to my business that I had no experience in.

I felt trapped and unable to change my circumstances. I needed to maintain the stability of my income, but maintaining the stability of my income meant I was working too much. It also meant I couldn't grow my business any further. I finally had to admit to myself that I was miserable.

It was a slow and painful realization, but I knew something had to change. I started identifying a target audience and strategically positioning myself to take control of my schedule. I realized that knowing your target audience and ideal client is far more important than I ever imagined.

I was able to shift my business and identify which clients to turn away and the right clients to take on. Each step was a strategic gain of time and replacement of income. In a few months, I had retired my brick-and-mortar computer repair business and was able to invest the money and time I saved back into the new direction I was heading.

I learned that their emotional connections, desires, and goals are crucial in making better business decisions, attracting the right clients, and setting yourself up for success. Once you map out your ideal client, you can create a solid business plan that includes your personal goals too.

My cautionary tale teaches the importance of knowing your target audience and ideal client, as it can make or break your business. And in my case, it made all the difference in the world. The lesson I learned the hard way is that having a clear and strategic understanding of your audience is crucial for success."

In the end, assuming everyone is your ideal client will result in missed opportunities, failed marketing campaigns, and a lack of meaningful connections with potential customers. It's crucial to identify and understand your target audience to effectively grow your business.

The Typical Scenario...

Typically, without a specified target audience, entrepreneurs and small business owners use broad marketing tactics such as mass advertising and general product offerings.

However, these solutions don't work very well because they do not effectively target the specific needs and preferences of any specific audience. As a result, the messaging and products fail to resonate with the intended audience, leading to missed opportunities for sales and growth.

Likewise, these solutions do not allow for personalized and tailored strategies that are crucial for establishing strong connections and relationships with potential clients.

To truly get past the assumption that everyone is your target audience, a more targeted and focused approach is required, such as identifying a specific target audience and creating personalized marketing strategies to appeal to their unique needs and preferences.

Just Do It Not

Avoid the mistake of assuming everyone is your client and just clearly identify your target audience right from the start. This is your best option because without a clear understanding of who your ideal audience is, you will waste time, money, and resources on marketing efforts that are simply not resonating with the right people.

And, as with Monte's example, you can waste time and cause yourself extra frustration by blindly serving everyone that comes your way. Stop taking on every single job simply because you can. Mapping out your ideal audience can help you determine which jobs are the right jobs for you.

To put this into immediate action, start by narrowing down your audience by identifying who has the most interest in your product or service. Do you have a client you wish you could clone?

Begin researching and understanding the interests of that ideal client. Then, create a detailed customer avatar to keep your specified target audience in mind with every decision you make for your business.

For example:

1. If you are a fitness entrepreneur, instead of marketing to everyone who wants to get fit, narrow down your target audience to women aged 25-45 who are interested in high-intensity interval training.

2. If you are a small business owner selling eco-friendly products, don't assume that everyone is your ideal client. Instead, focus on marketing to environmentally conscious consumers who prioritize sustainable living.

3. As a tech startup founder, identify your target audience as small businesses looking for affordable and user-friendly software solutions, rather than trying to appeal to every business regardless of their needs.

4. For a photography business, instead of assuming everyone is your ideal client, narrow down your target audience to engaged couples looking for wedding photography to capture their special day.

By clearly identifying your target audience and tailoring your marketing efforts to reach them specifically, you will have avoided or fixed the mistake of assuming everyone is your client. This will ultimately lead to more effective and efficient business development for all your entrepreneurial endeavors.

Are You Taking on Clients, You Wish You Hadn't?
But what if you've already been doing it? How can you fix an assumption that everyone is your client, or if you have simply been disregarding a target audience completely?

Business development is the key.

1. Do relevant market research to identify your ideal audience and understand their needs and pain points. Use this information to craft targeted marketing messages and strategies.

2. Build partnerships with other businesses that cater to your ideal audience. This can help you gain access to a wider customer base and increase your business's visibility.

3. Refine your products or services to better fit the needs of your ideal audience. This might involve adjusting your offerings or creating new products specifically tailored to their needs.

4. Create targeted content and advertising campaigns that speak directly to your ideal audience. This can help you establish a strong connection with your target market and increase the likelihood of converting leads into customers.

Once You Start, You'll Take It to Heart

To prevent the mistake of assuming everyone is your ideal client, it's crucial to clearly define your target audience. Identify their characteristics, interests, and pain points, and tailor your marketing efforts to address their specific needs.

By focusing on a specific demographic, you can better understand and connect with your ideal audience, leading to more effective and successful business development initiatives.

Helpful Resources

- **The Ideal Client Map online companion members area** – Chapter 1
  - ➢ Register Your Book Here: https://register.theidealclientmap.com
  - ➢ Access Resources here: https://resources.theidealclientmap.com

- **The Ideal Client Map – Printable PNG File**
  - ➢ The Ideal Client Map Online Training: Get the Mind Map and the Training to use it. Save tons of frustration identifying your Ideal Client Avatar.
  - ➢ http://mapyouridealclient.com
  - ➢ Read the book "Copywriting Secrets" by Jim Edwards.

Monte's #1 Piece of Advice

Here's my biggest advice on this issue do not cater to everyone.

It's crucial for entrepreneurs and small business owners to clearly identify their target audience and tailor their products and services to meet the specific needs and preferences of that audience.

Identifying and understanding your target audience is essential for the long-term success of your business.

- It allows you to focus on the clients that give you the highest return.
- It means your marketing efforts and resources are spent on the most receptive and profitable demographic.

By understanding the unique characteristics and behaviors of your target audience, you can develop products and services that truly resonate with them and address their pain points.

This focused approach will not only attract more customers, but also lead to greater customer satisfaction and loyalty. Stop assuming that everyone is in your target audience - take the time to identify and understand your ideal audience for long-term business success.

What We Covered

- Define your target audience
- Identify their characteristics, interests, and pain points
- Tailor marketing efforts to address specific needs

What Did We Learn?

****True/False Questions:****

1. **True/False:** Assuming everyone is your client can lead to generalized marketing efforts that are less effective.

2. **True/False:** Narrowing your target audience helps in creating more focused and efficient business development strategies.

3. **True/False:** Personalized and tailored strategies are not necessary for establishing strong connections with potential clients.

4. **True/False:** Identifying a specific target audience can help in avoiding the frustration of catering to irrelevant customer requests.

****Multiple Choice Questions:****

1. **What is one of the primary reasons why assuming everyone is your client spells disaster for a business?**
   A. It attracts a large number of potential clients.
   B. It leads to scattered and unfocused marketing efforts.
   C. It saves time and resources.
   D. It simplifies business operations.

2. **Entrepreneurs often fall into the trap of assuming everyone is their client due to:**
   A. An overabundance of confidence.
   B. Lack of competition in the market.
   C. Fear of missing out on potential customers.
   D. Detailed understanding of their target audience.

3. **What stage of a business is most prone to the mistake of assuming everyone is a client?**
   A. During economic downturns.
   B. When the business is planning for retirement.
   C. At the early stages of development.
   D. After decades of being in the market.

4. **To fix the mistake of assuming everyone is your client, you should:**
   A. Stop marketing your products altogether.
   B. Partner with irrelevant businesses.
   C. Conduct relevant market research to identify your ideal audience.
   D. Provide generic products and services.

Fill-in-the-Blanks Questions:

1. To efficiently cater to your customers, it's essential to create a detailed ________________ to understand their interests and needs.

2. Taking on every job without considering if it fits your ideal audience can lead to wasted ________________ and ____________.

3. One effective strategy to refine your marketing efforts is to build partnerships with other businesses that cater to your ________________.

4. Personalized and targeted _____________ and ______ _____campaigns can help establish a strong connection with your ideal audience.

Find the Answer Key in the Online Companion Members Area

While assuming everyone is their ideal client can be a common mistake, it is equally essential to avoid casting too wide of a net when identifying your target audience. In the following chapter, we will explore how focusing on too broad of a target audience can lead to diluted messaging and ultimately hinder the success of your marketing efforts. Keep reading to learn how to effectively narrow down your target audience for more impactful communication.

"One Size Does Not Fit All"

Don't Assume a Target Audience is the Same as An Ideal Client

Target Audience versus Ideal Client

You have likely heard the importance of identifying your target audience and ideal client. However, it is a common mistake to assume that these two terms are one and the same. In fact, the reality is that a target audience and an ideal client are not interchangeable concepts, and it is crucial to understand the difference between the two in order to effectively grow your business.

Imagine this: you're at a crowded party, trying to strike up a conversation. Your goal is to connect with someone on a deeper level, to find that perfect match who shares your interests, values, and sense of humor. In the world of marketing, your target audience is like the entire party – a diverse group of people with varied interests and backgrounds. Sure, they all share enough in common to be at the same party, but your ideal client? That's the person you're searching for, the one who lights up when you start talking about your passion and just gets you. See the difference?

For the longest time, I mistakenly believed that my target audience and ideal client were one and the same. It wasn't until I dug deeper into the concept of defining my ideal client that I discovered the distinction. They're definitely related, but they're certainly not duplicates. The internet often muddies the waters by using these terms interchangeably, but trust me when I say, they're not the same.

Instead of trying to cast a wide net over a generic target audience, really focus on creating a specific ideal client avatar. This will allow you to form a more meaningful connection with the individuals who are most likely to resonate with your message. Do the work to identify and understand your ideal client, and you'll find that your marketing efforts become more targeted, more effective, and more rewarding. Trust me, the effort is worth it for the deeper connections and more impactful results.

Assuming that a target audience is the same as the different ideal clients it contains fails to recognize the unique needs, behaviors, and preferences of individual people within the target audience. By not understanding this distinction, you risk wasting the same time, resources, and energy as if you hadn't defined the target audience in the first place.

There are two main reasons behind why people make this mistake.

- First, the pressure to appeal to a broad audience can result in a focus on quantity over quality, leading to 'not seeing the trees because of the forest'.

- Second, there is a tendency to generalize and oversimplify a customer base, assuming that they all have the same needs.

This mistake tends to occur during the business development and marketing strategies process. In the rush to reach a larger audience and generate more leads, it can be tempting to gloss over the nuances and complexities of individual ideal clients. However, this approach ultimately hinders your ability to effectively communicate your value proposition and build meaningful relationships with the clients who are most likely to benefit from your products or services.

Don't overlook the different types of trees in the forest. Identify the ideal clients in that target audience. Focus on developing a deep understanding of their ideal clients. This involves conducting the right market research to identify the specific needs, pain points, and preferences of different segments within their target audience. By creating detailed buyer avatars businesses can tailor their messaging, offerings, and customer experience to better meet the unique needs of their most valuable clients.

Consequences:
The consequences of making this mistake include wasting time and resources on marketing to the wrong audience, failing to connect with potential customers, and ultimately losing out on sales and revenue. Additionally, it can lead to

a lack of brand loyalty, negative reputation, and missed opportunities for growth.

These consequences are much worse than you think because they not only affect your current business success, but they also impact your long-term viability. Failing to properly identify and target ideal clients can lead to a significant decrease in profitability, hinder your ability to expand and innovate, attract more time wasting customers, and could ultimately result in the failure of your business.

Therefore, it is essential to thoroughly understand the intricacies of your target audience and the different ideal clients it contains in order to effectively tailor your marketing strategies and maximize your business potential.

Typically Speaking...

Most entrepreneurs and small business owners don't even realize they have made the mistake of assuming a target audience is the same thing as the different ideal clients it contains. Unfortunately, this holds them back because they fail to address the unique needs and preferences of individual ideal clients. Using a one-size-fits-all approach resonates with fewer people, inspires less business, and the business it does attract is not ideal.

The Only Way to Avoid This Mistake

Honestly, the only solution to the assumption that a target audience is the same thing as an ideal client is to stop thinking that way. You absolutely need to accurately and precisely develop an Ideal Client Avatar.

Developing an Ideal Client Avatar allows you to truly understand the diverse needs and preferences of your ideal clients within your target audience. By segmenting your market and identifying specific customer avatars, you can tailor your products, services, and marketing strategies to effectively meet the unique needs of each ideal client.

To put this solution into immediate action, start by conducting relevant market research to gather data on your target audience. Use this data to create customer avatars that represent the different ideal clients within your market. Then, tailor your products, services, and marketing messages to speak directly to the needs and preferences of each customer avatar.

Examples of this solution in action in the real world:

1. **A clothing retailer conducts market research and customer segmentation to identify three distinct customer avatars:** fashion-forward millennials, budget-conscious parents, and luxury shoppers. They then create specific marketing campaigns and product offerings tailored to each avatar, resulting in increased sales and customer satisfaction.

2. **A software company identifies two key customer avatars within their target audience:** small business owners looking for affordable solutions and

enterprise-level IT professionals seeking advanced features. By developing targeted product packages and marketing messages for each avatar, they effectively meet the needs of both customer segments and drive revenue growth

3. **A health and wellness coach conducts market research and customer segmentation to identify four distinct customer avatars:** fitness enthusiasts, busy professionals, new moms, and retirees. They then customize their coaching programs and content to address the unique needs and challenges of each avatar, leading to higher client retention and referral rates.

4. **A marketing agency uses customer segmentation to identify three distinct customer avatars within their target audience:** marketing managers seeking strategic support, small business owners looking for affordable services, and enterprise-level executives in need of comprehensive solutions. By tailoring their service offerings and proposals to each avatar, they successfully attract and retain clients across different market segments.

What if you have been thinking this way since day one?
But what if you've already made this mistake? Fortunately, there are ways to fix it through smart business development strategies. One approach is to conduct that market research we mentioned earlier. This way you can

better understand the different segments within your target audience, helping you tailor your products or services to meet the specific needs of each customer group.

In the real world, we see this in action with companies like Nike, who have different lines of products targeting specific customer segments such as athletes, casual consumers, and fashion-forward individuals. Another example is in the hospitality industry, where hotels and resorts target different experiences and amenities to attract a specific kind of guest, whether that be business travelers or vacationers.

Another solution is to consider forming strategic partnerships with other businesses that cater to your ideal clients for different reasons. By collaborating with these partners, you can share your customer bases for a win/win situation.

Helpful Resources:

- **The Ideal Client Map online companion members area** – Chapter 2
  - ➢ Register Your Book Here: https://register.theidealclientmap.com
  - ➢ Access Resources here: https://resources.theidealclientmap.com
  - ➢ How to start using The Ideal Client Map PNG File
  - ➢ Mind Mapping – Mindomo: https://www.mindomo.com/#j-cEsK7I-0
    by the way, TICM is a mind map / flow chart /

visual aid / focus tool / and all around best way to clearly develop an Ideal Client Avatar.

  - Read the book "Unlock Your Ideal Customer Avatar Profile: 10 Fatal Mistakes To Avoid When Connecting with Your Target Audience... No Matter What You Sell" by Jim Edwards.

- **TICM Online Training:** The Ideal Client Map Online Training is a visual tool and training that helps you 'see' the emotional relationships of your Ideal Client Avatar.
  - Without a visual tool it takes a **ton of brain power** to keep all the data, and the emotional relationships, on '**top of mind**'.
  - Stop using words to keep track of emotions and the emotional triggers.
  - **Start using visuals to make it easy.** https://mapyouridealclient.com

Monte's #1 Piece of Advice

I highly recommend, no, I URGE you to accurately nail down your target audience and precisely dial in your most prominent Ideal Client Avatar before making any further business decisions. The biggest mistake entrepreneurs and small business owners can make in business development is assuming that their target audience is a homogenous group.

When crafting a marketing message, understanding that your target audience is a subset of a larger demographic is fundamental. Indeed, this audience is not a monolithic entity; it's composed of different members, each with unique personalities and characteristics. Even as we define our ideal customer avatars, we must recognize that a shared trait among group members does not equate to uniform behavior or preferences. As each member of your target audience carries a distinct blend of experiences and attitudes, they interact with your brand through their individualized lens.

Acknowledging the diversity within your target audience entails examining the varying traits among its members. While certain characteristics might appear to make some individuals a marketer's dream, it is crucial to delve deeper. Each trait presents a different influence and significance; what may serve as a primary motivator for one person could be a secondary concern for another. This variance is much like how individuals with both arachnophobia and hydrophobia might react differently when faced with a spider or a body of water. Their actions will depend on their personal hierarchy of fears and rational decision-making processes, despite sharing common phobias. Thus, to truly connect with your audience, one must appreciate that people with identical traits will still process information and make decisions in their unique ways. This is why precise targeting and segmentation are indispensable—to tailor communications that resonate on an individual level. For instance, some might be impulsive, preferring immediate action over analysis, whereas others undertake a meticulous evaluation of risks and outcomes. By accounting for these nuances, a savvy entrepreneur or marketer can engage more genuinely with each subset of their audience, crafting messages that reflect an understanding of their specific character and needs.

This is so important because trying to appeal to a broad, generic target audience will only lead to diluted marketing efforts and missed opportunities to truly connect with and serve your ideal clients. By focusing on the specific segments within your target audience that matter the most, you can tailor your products, services, and marketing strategies to address their unique needs and effectively differentiate yourself from competitors.

Take action right away on what you've learned in this chapter by thoroughly defining the most important ideal client segment within your target audience. Develop detailed buyer avatars for each relevant segment and create personalized marketing strategies to address their specific needs and preferences. By doing so, you can position your business for long-term success and sustainable growth.

In a Nutshell

- Don't assume your target audience is the same as your ideal clients

- Identify your target audience and accurately define the ideal clients that matter the most

- Conduct relevant market research and customer segmentation

- Understand the diverse needs and preferences of your ideal clients

- Tailor business development strategies to reach and engage with each segment

- Ensure you are meeting the specific needs of your primary ideal client for greater success

What Did We Learn?
****True/False Questions:****

1. **True or False:** A target audience encompasses the overall demographic that might be interested in your product, while an ideal client is a very specific subset of this audience with particular characteristics.

2. **True or False:** It is sufficient to market to a broad target audience without creating a specific ideal client avatar.

3. **True or False:** Failing to differentiate between your target audience and ideal clients can lead to wasted resources and missed sales opportunities.

4. **True or False**: Generalizing and assuming all customers have the same needs is a common mistake in developing business marketing strategies.

Multiple Choice Questions:

1. **Which of the following best describes an Ideal Client Avatar?**
   A. A general representation of the entire target audience.
   B. A detailed and specific representation of an ideal client within the target audience.
   C. A competitor's client profile.
   D. A fictional character used in advertising.

2. **Why is it important to conduct market research when developing an Ideal Client Avatar?**
   A. To understand the overall market size.
   B. To gather data on specific needs, pain points, and preferences of different segments.
   C. To reduce advertising costs.
   D. To attract attention from competitors.

3. **What happens if you fail to properly identify and target your ideal clients?**
   A. Increase in brand loyalty.
   B. Attraction of irresponsive customers.
   C. Savings in marketing efforts.
   D. Increase in sales and revenue.

4. **Which of these is a smart business development strategy to address the mistake of not differentiating between target audience and ideal clients?**
   A. Ignoring market research.
   B. Conducting comprehensive market research.
   C. Broadening your marketing messages.
   D. Avoiding partnership opportunities.

Fill-in-the-Blank Questions:

1. Marketing efforts become more targeted, effective, and rewarding when businesses create ____________ to understand their ideal client.

2. The consequence of targeting a generic audience rather than specific ideal clients may result in a lack of ___________________________to your brand.

3. Failing to address unique preferences of individual ideal clients generally leads to missing _____________ ____________for business growth.

4. Developing an Ideal Client Avatar helps businesses _ ________________________ their products, services, and marketing strategies to meet the unique needs of each ideal client.

Find the Answer Key in the Online Companion Members Area

As we have seen, assuming a target audience is homogenous can lead to missed opportunities and ineffective marketing strategies. In the following chapter, we will explore the critical mistake of rushing the process of defining ideal clients, and the importance of taking the time to gather comprehensive insights to truly understand and connect with them. Keep reading to discover how this vital step can transform your marketing approach and drive success.

"The False Start"

The High Price of Rushing Through Your Ideal Client Avatar

Rushing the process of developing your ideal client is a mistake that is imperative to avoid.

As an entrepreneur or small business owner, the process of defining your ideal client avatar is an essential aspect of business development.

However, one of the most common mistakes that many individuals make is rushing through this process instead of taking the time to gather the right comprehensive insights. This mistake can have a significant impact on the success and growth of your business.

Rushing the process of defining your ideal client instead of taking the time to gather comprehensive insights is a mistake because it can lead to a misalignment between your products or services and the needs and preferences of your target market. When you don't take the time to truly understand your ideal client, you run the risk of investing time and resources into strategies that just don't resonate with your target audience.

Several reason account for this mistake.

First, there is often a sense of urgency to start generating revenue and acquiring customers as quickly as possible, leading to a rushed approach to defining the ideal client.

Second, some individuals underestimate the importance of understanding their target market in detail and believe they can rely on general assumptions or stereotypes.

Lastly, the process of defining an ideal client can be challenging and time-consuming, leading some to take shortcuts in the hopes of expediting the process.

This mistake tends to occur in the early stages of business development when entrepreneurs and small business owners are eager to get their products or services in front of potential customers. They may feel pressure to start marketing and selling before fully understanding who their ideal client is. Additionally, as businesses evolve and enter new markets, there may be a temptation to rush through the ideal client avatar process to keep up with the pace of growth.

Consequences:
By not taking the time to gather comprehensive insights, you risk targeting the wrong audience, wasting valuable resources on ineffective marketing and sales efforts, and ultimately damaging your brand reputation.

These consequences are much worse than you think because targeting the wrong audience can result in low conversion rates, missed opportunities, and a negative impact on your bottom line. Rushing this process can also lead to a lack of understanding of your target market's needs, making it difficult to develop products or services that truly resonate with them.

Monte's Story: The Time I Wasted Tons of Time and Effort Developing Services No One Wanted (even for free)

At some point during my business journey, I decided to diversify my income streams. I was driven by the ambition to grow my earnings without having to continually chase new clients. I aimed to increase the value I provided to my existing clients, figuring that expanding my range of services would be the ideal path.

This approach seemed like a smart strategy given the relationships I had already built with my client base.

Eager to implement my plan, I invested in state-of-the-art video creating software. I was enthusiastic and consumed by the potential of video ads, which I understood could be a powerful tool. I was on a mission to become proficient in creating compelling video advertisements and saw clear benefits for my clients. Surely, these engaging visuals would skyrocket their social media presence and overall business visibility. My ideas brimmed with confidence and conviction.

The idea was simple: offer comprehensive ad packages to my existing clients. In my mind, this wouldn't just diversify my income; it would also significantly benefit my clients by enhancing their online engagement. With this dual goal in mind, I began to craft my video ads, envisioning enthusiastic responses from those I had served so well over the years. I genuinely believed this could be a win-win situation, both for my clients and myself.

Little did I know that not one of my clients had the slightest interest in expanding their social media footprint. Despite my excitement, energy, and effort, it was baffling to see my offerings met with complete indifference. This culminated in one of the most surprising lessons of my entrepreneurial journey. I had assumed that the value I saw in video ads would naturally be apparent to my clients as well.

In an attempt to spark interest, I even offered to create video ads for established clients free of charge, hoping the results would speak for themselves and create demand.

Remarkably, not a single client took me up on my offer. It wasn't that they doubted the quality of what I produced—they never even saw it. Their reluctance had nothing to do with the ads themselves.

The real revelation came when I understood why they were unconcerned with advertising. They were already overwhelmed with more business than their current teams could manage. With the local job market sparse and finding reliable employees being incredibly challenging, expanding their customer base further via social media was the last thing on their minds.

In hindsight, it's clear that my clients were not the right market for video ads. Ultimately, I spent countless hours learning, refining, and honing my video creation skills to no avail. The crucial mistake was not mapping out my ideal client for these services or conducting thorough market research.

If I had only mapped out my clients' current needs and capabilities ahead of time, I could have avoided investing so much effort into a proposition that ultimately fell flat. This experience now stands as a valuable lesson in aligning new offerings with client readiness and market demands.

In the competitive world of business development, taking the time to define your ideal client is crucial for success. It's essential to gather comprehensive insights to ensure that you are effectively targeting the right audience and meeting their needs. Rushing this process can have terrible, horrible, life-ruining consequences for entrepreneurs and small business owners.

Typical Strategies That Don't Really Work...

Entrepreneurs and small business owners often use limited basic demographic research and broad market segmentation. These tactics don't work very well because they only provide surface-level understanding of the target audience and fail to capture the nuanced needs and desires of the ideal client. Without a deep understanding of the ideal client, businesses are unable to tailor their products or services to effectively meet the specific needs of their target market.

Additionally, these solutions lack the necessary depth to create targeted marketing strategies that resonate with the ideal client, leading to wasted time and resources on ineffective marketing efforts. In order to truly fix the mistake, entrepreneurs and small business owners need to invest in in-depth market research, customer interviews, and data analysis to gain comprehensive insights into their ideal client. This approach ensures that businesses can accurately identify their ideal client and develop tailored strategies to effectively engage and serve them.

How to Avoid, Fix, or Prevent Making This Mistake
The #1 solution to avoid rushing the process of defining your ideal client is to gather relevant comprehensive insights before making any decisions. This is the best option because it allows you to truly understand your target audience and tailor your products or services to meet their specific needs and preferences.

To put this into immediate action, start by conducting the right market research to gather data on your target demographic. Use surveys, interviews, and customer feedback to gain insights into their behaviors, preferences, and pain points. Analyze this data to create detailed buyer avatars that represent your ideal clients, including their demographics, interests, and buying habits.

In the real world, this solution looks like:

1. A fitness entrepreneur who takes the time to understand the specific needs and goals of their target audience before creating a new workout program, resulting in higher client satisfaction and retention.

2. A small business owner who conducts market research to gather insights into the buying habits and preferences of their ideal clients, allowing them to tailor their marketing campaigns and product offerings to better meet their needs.

3. A beauty brand that invests in customer feedback and surveys to gather insights into the preferences and concerns of their target demographic, leading to the development of new products that resonate with their audience.

4. An e-commerce entrepreneur who analyzes customer data to better understand the shopping behaviors and preferences of their ideal clients, allowing them to optimize their website and product offerings to enhance the overall customer experience.

What if you have already rushed through the development process?

Don't worry, if you have already made this mistake, there are steps you can take to fix it. Begin by conducting in-depth market research and data analysis. This will provide comprehensive insights into their target audience, allowing them to refine their ideal client profile and better understand the needs and preferences of their potential customers.

Furthermore, utilizing customer feedback and conducting surveys can provide invaluable information about their target market. By actively seeking input from their audience, entrepreneurs can gain a better understanding of their ideal client and tailor their products or services to meet the needs of their customers more effectively.

Another important step to fixing this mistake is to engage in networking and build relationships with potential clients. By establishing personal connections and actively listening to their needs and challenges, entrepreneurs can gain further insights into their ideal client and adapt their business strategies accordingly.

Finally, entrepreneurs can benefit from seeking professional advice and guidance from business development experts. These professionals can offer valuable insights and recommendations for refining the ideal client profile and developing targeted marketing strategies based on comprehensive data and analysis.

By implementing these strategies, entrepreneurs and small business owners can effectively fix the mistake of rushing the process of defining their ideal client and take proactive steps to gather comprehensive insights and understanding their target market more deeply.

Examples of this in action in the real world:

1. A small business owner in the fashion industry **conducts detailed market research and engages in customer feedback surveys** to refine their ideal client profile and develop personalized marketing strategies based on consumer insights.

2. An entrepreneur in the technology sector actively networks with potential clients and **seeks professional guidance to better understand the needs and preferences of their target market**, leading to the development of tailored products and services.

3. A start-up company in the food and beverage industry **utilizes data analysis and customer feedback to gain comprehensive insights into their ideal client**, allowing them to adapt their business strategies and product offerings to meet the specific needs of their target audience.

4. A marketing agency seeks professional advice from business development experts to **refine their ideal client profile and develop targeted marketing strategies** based on comprehensive data and analysis, leading to more effective client acquisition and retention.

Helpful Resources:

- **The Ideal Client Map online companion members area** – Chapter 3
  - Register Your Book Here: https://register.theidealclientmap.com
  - Access Resources here: https://resources.theidealclientmap.com
  - Where Feature-Benefit-Meaning plugs into TICM

- The Ideal Client Map Training:
  The 5 Questions Bonus Training helps identify the Feature-Benefit-Meaning connections, so you resonate with your target audience better than strings on a guitar.
  http://mapyouridealclient.com

Monte's #1 Piece of Advice

Here's my biggest advice on this issue: Do not rush any part in the process of developing your Ideal Client Avatar. It is crucial to take the time to gather comprehensive insights before moving forward with your business development.

Defining your ideal client is one of the most important steps in building a successful business. Rushing this process can lead to targeting the wrong audience, which can result in wasted time and resources. By taking the time to gather comprehensive insights about your target market, you can better understand their needs, pain points, and preferences, allowing you to tailor your products and services to better meet their needs.

Remember, the success of your business depends on your ability to connect with your ideal client. By rushing the process of defining your ideal client, you may miss out on valuable opportunities to truly understand and connect with your target audience. Taking the time to gather comprehensive insights will ultimately lead to more effective marketing strategies, stronger customer relationships, and increased business success.

I encourage you to take action on what you've learned in this chapter. Take the time to thoroughly research and analyze your target market and use the insights you gather to define your ideal client in a way that will set your business up for long-term success.

Let's Summarize

- Take time to gather comprehensive insights
- Conduct market research and analyze customer behavior
- Gather feedback from existing clients
- Ensure clear understanding of target audience
- Tailor products and services to meet specific needs

What Did We Learn?

****True/False Questions****

1. Rushing the process of defining your ideal client can lead to a misalignment between your products and the needs of your target market.

2. General assumptions or stereotypes are sufficient for understanding your target market.

3. The ideal client avatar process should be revisited as businesses evolve or enter new markets.

4. Limited basic demographic research is enough to create effective marketing strategies.

****Multiple Choice Questions****

1. **What is a common mistake entrepreneurs make regarding defining their ideal client?**
   A. Investing too much time
   B. Rushing through the process
   C. Ignoring marketing altogether
   D. Exclusively focusing on new products

2. **Which of the following is an effective way to gather comprehensive insights on your ideal client?**
   A. Guessing based on trends
   B. Using only demographic data
   C. Conducting customer interviews and surveys
   D. Relying on competitors' strategies

3. **What is a negative consequence of targeting the wrong audience?**
   A. Decreased product variety
   B. High conversion rates
   C. Wasting resources on ineffective marketing
   D. Enhanced brand reputation

4. **How can entrepreneurs build relationships to understand their ideal clients better?**
   A. Ignoring customer feedback
   B. Networking and listening to client needs
   C. Increasing prices arbitrarily
   D. Focusing solely on internal ideas

Fill-in-the-Blanks Questions

1. Entrepreneurs often make the mistake of rushing through the process of defining their ideal client due to a sense of _______________ to start generating revenue.

2. Investing in in-depth market research, customer interviews, and data analysis helps to gain _________ insights into the ideal client.

3. Conducting surveys and actively seeking __________ from their audience helps entrepreneurs understand their ideal client better.

4. To avoid the drawbacks of broad market segmentation, small business owners should create detailed buyer ____________.

Find the Answer Key in the Online Companion Members Area

As the previous chapter emphasized, rushing the process of defining the ideal client can lead to critical oversights. In the following chapter, we will delve into the mistake of neglecting to define specific demographics and psychographics, highlighting the importance of gaining a comprehensive understanding of your target audience. Keep reading to discover the impact of this crucial aspect of client development.

"The Invisible Audience"

Neglecting to Define the Who and the Why of Your Target Market

Relevant Demographics and Psychographics Are a Strategic Necessity.

In the world of business development, one of the most critical mistakes that entrepreneurs and small business owners can make is neglecting to define the specific demographics and psychographics that are relevant for their target market. This involves **failing to identify the specific characteristics and behaviors** of the groups and individuals that are most likely to be interested in and purchasing your products or services.

Let's talk a little bit about how neglecting those boring old demographics and elusive emotional psychographics in your marketing is a big mistake. At its core, **this oversight can lead to wasted time, money, and effort.** By not clearly understanding your target market, you risk creating marketing strategies and products that don't resonate with the people who are most likely to buy from you. In essence, **you're throwing your resources at an invisible audience.**

And check this out, being unclear about your target market's way of thinking wastes time. That's because you will incorrectly anticipate, assume, and prepare for things that aren't necessary. I've seen this done by clients and I've even done this plenty of times myself. Things such as preparing quotes, offers, or proposals that fell on deaf ears or worse, repelled my client because they felt I didn't truly understand their needs.

Many folks make this mistake for a few key reasons.

1. **Unfocused Approach to Customer Acquisition:** As I have previously mentioned in prior chapters, it's common to cast a wide net to try and appeal to the largest number of people possible.

2. **Lack of Understanding:** Some entrepreneurs just don't realize the importance of targeting specific demographics and psychographics, leading to a lack of prioritization in this area.

3. **Fear of Missing Out:** Business owners often feel that defining specific demographics and psychographics will limit their potential customer base, when in reality, the opposite is true.

This mistake starts to rear its head at the early stages of business development when entrepreneurs and small business owners are eager to get their products or services into the market as quickly as possible. Often, there's a rush to launch without taking the necessary time to truly understand and define who their ideal customers are.

Consequences:
You may be thinking that defining specific demographics and psychographics for your business development simply plays a minor role. But the major consequences of this mistake are much worse than you think.

Without a clear understanding of who your ideal customers are, you won't be able to correctly tailor your products or services to meet their specific needs and desires. This will result in lukewarm customer feedback, no referrals, and mediocre sales.

Furthermore, by not clearly and accurately identifying your target market, **you will waste valuable time and resources** marketing to the wrong audience. You'll end up with low conversion rates, high customer acquisition costs, **the wrong time-sucking clients**, and ultimately, a struggling business.

Why I Decided to Say 'No' to Referrals and Take Back Control of My Business
Picture this: It's another typical morning in my tech repair haven, where I, Monte, am whizzing through work, solving computer conundrums left and right. Business was good—no, it was great.

For several years, I'd been the go-to guy for local individuals and businesses with computer hiccups. Most jobs were straightforward: fix the issue, get the handshake, and move on to the next task. Life was humming along smoothly. This all happened before my Chapter 1 story of when I realized I hated my business.

One fine day, my phone rings. It's a local bank manager. They've got a proposition: can I help their customers whose computers have been compromised by scammers? These folks needed their computers scrubbed clean or else the bank couldn't reactivate their online banking privileges, and they were in quite the pickle. "Absolutely," I said, not just willing, but eager to help. I imagined a stream of clients and an influx of goodwill speeding my way.

Being an enterprising sort, I didn't stop there. Armed with my best smile and a stack of business cards, I visited several other banks to propose the same deal. Soon enough, the referrals started to roll in. My calendar filled up, my business boomed, and I felt like I was on top of the world. Helping people and growing my business? A win-win.

Then came the twist. The referrals were mostly elderly clients who had been scammed because they struggled with even the basics of computer use. Sweet, humble, and utterly bewildered by technology, they needed far more than just a quick fix. Many couldn't make it to my shop, meaning I had to trek out to their homes. And these visits? They were anything but short.

Suddenly, my days were consumed with driving from one location to another, dealing with endless complications.

Each service call stretched far beyond its initial scope—resetting passwords, navigating through endless security questions, and explaining each step in great detail. I was practically providing a personalized tutorial on basic computer use.

Responsibilities piled high. The once-smooth flow of my business turned into a chaotic mess. My beloved regular clients—those steady, low-maintenance businesses—were feeling neglected. They deserved my attention and expertise, and I was failing to deliver. I started losing sleep, stressed out from running too many trains on the track.

As if things couldn't get worse, one day I received a scathing 1-star review. A frustrated scam victim demanded I help recover their stolen email account without any extra charge.

When I explained that this additional service required a new invoice, they were furious. The result? A nasty slap of a review that stung more than I thought possible.

That review was my wake-up call. It dawned on me that, despite my best intentions, these scam victims were not my Ideal Clients. The time and energy spent on them was draining my business dry. I couldn't keep up; my regular clients, the backbone of my business, were paying the price.

I had to make a tough decision. I contacted all the banks and informed them that I could no longer accept new clients from their referrals. Polite yet firm, I took back my business cards and put a halt to what had become a downward spiral.

Looking back, the lesson was clear as crystal. Had I developed my Ideal Client Avatar from the get-go, I could have steered clear of the fraud victims and avoided turning my life into a circus. Instead, I would have preserved my energy and resources, channeling them into more efficient and profitable activities.

Every business has its Ideal Client, and finding yours is like finding gold. It can save you from the pitfalls of misguided ventures and ensure your efforts are invested in the right direction. Trust me, it's a discovery well worth the effort. In the competitive world of business, not knowing your Ideal Client Avatar's demographics and psychographics can lead to missed opportunities, the wrong jobs, and ultimately the decline of your company. Don't underestimate the importance of dialing in your target audience – it could make or break your success.

#1 Way to Avoid This Mistake

Avoid this mistake with ease by conducting some relevant market research right away. This solution is the best option because it provides crucial information about your target audience, allowing you to tailor your products and marketing strategies accordingly.

To put this solution into immediate action, start by identifying some relevant demographics for your target audience. Use surveys and email campaigns to gather info about their psychographics and analyze the data to gain insights into your customers' thoughts, preferences, and purchasing patterns.

Here are four detailed, practical examples of how to put this solution into action in the real world:

1. A clothing brand conducts market research to define their target audience as **young adults aged 18-30 who are fashion-conscious and environmentally conscious.** They use this information to create a sustainable fashion line that resonates with their target demographic.

2. A local coffee shop conducts market research to understand their customers' preferences and discovers that their **target audience values convenience and quality.** As a result, they introduce a mobile app for easy ordering and loyalty rewards program to attract and retain customers.

3. A software company conducts market research to **identify the industries and businesses that would benefit most from their product.** They use this information to create targeted marketing

campaigns and personalized sales pitches to effectively reach and convert their ideal customers.

4. A fitness studio conducts market research to understand the demographics and psychographics of their target audience, **realizing that there is a demand for high-intensity interval training classes among young professionals.** They pivot their class offerings to cater to this demand and see an increase in class attendance and customer satisfaction.

How To Turn the Situation Around

But what if you've already skipped identifying the demographics and psychographics of your ideal audience? No worries! You can still fix it with strong business development strategies.

Start by conducting demographic and psychographic market research to gain a better understanding of your customer base. From there, create targeted marketing materials and campaigns that speak directly to the needs and desires of your ideal customer. Additionally, you can refine your product or service offerings to better meet the needs of your target audience. Finally, don't be afraid to pivot and adjust your strategies based on the feedback and data you receive.

Here are four detailed, practical examples of how this can be put into action in the real world:

1. A boutique fitness studio realizes that their current marketing efforts aren't yielding the desired results. After conducting market research, they discover that their target audience is primarily **busy working professionals who value convenience and flexibility.** They restructure their class schedule to better accommodate their customers' needs and launch a targeted marketing campaign highlighting the convenience of their location and schedule.

2. A small tech startup is struggling to gain traction with their new product. After analyzing their sales data, they realize that the majority of their customers are **tech-savvy millennials who are early adopters of new technology.** They pivot their marketing efforts to focus on social media platforms and tech blogs, and they also provide educational content to help their customers understand the value of their product.

3. A local restaurant is facing declining sales and increased competition. After surveying their current customer base, they discover that the majority of their **patrons are health-conscious individuals who are looking for healthier dining options.** They revamp their menu to include more nutritious and lighter options, and they launch a marketing

campaign highlighting their commitment to providing healthy and delicious food choices.

4. An online beauty retailer is struggling to stand out in a crowded market. After analyzing their customer feedback, they realize that their **audience is passionate about cruelty-free and environmentally friendly beauty products.** They update their product offerings to include more sustainable and eco-friendly options, and they create a marketing strategy that emphasizes their commitment to ethical and sustainable beauty.

You Can Prevent This Mistake from Ever Happening Again

Now you know. Simply avoid the mistake of audience neglect by conducting thorough and relevant market research as soon as possible. Be sure to understand the needs, desires, and behaviors of your target audience, and segment them into specific groups based on common characteristics.

Develop specific Ideal Client Avatars for each group. Use this information to tailor your products, services, and marketing efforts to effectively reach and resonate with these different segments.

Continually reassess and update your target audience profiles and your Ideal Client Avatars as your business evolves, ensuring that you stay aligned with the needs and preferences of your customers.

By staying diligent in defining and understanding the specific demographics and psychographics that matter, you can avoid the costly mistake of marketing to an invisible audience.

Helpful Resources

- **The Ideal Client Map online companion members area** – Chapter 4
  - Register Your Book Here: https://register.theidealclientmap.com
  - Access Resources here: https://resources.theidealclientmap.com
  - 101 Questions to Create your Ideal Client Avatar https://www.influenceherdigitalmarketingsolutions.com/101questions
  - Plug the most relevant information from the 101 questions workbook into TICM

Monte's #1 Piece of Advice

Here's my biggest advice on this issue: **Map out the relevant demographics and psychographics with a visual map.** It is crucial to know exactly how your target audience is thinking, what they are saying in their heads, and see the context to effectively market and sell your products or services.

Defining specific demographics and psychographics is important because it allows you to tailor your marketing efforts to the needs and interests of your ideal customers.

Without this understanding, you may waste time and resources targeting the wrong audience or fail to appeal to the right demographic. By knowing your audience better than they know themselves, you can create personalized marketing campaigns that resonate with potential customers and ultimately lead to higher conversion rates and sales.

Now that you understand the significance of defining specific demographics and psychographics, it's time to put it into action. Grab the 101 Questions Workbook. (See the Helpful Resources section above.) Use this information to create detailed customer Avatars and develop targeted marketing strategies that speak directly to the needs and desires of your ideal customers. By doing so, you'll position your business for success and set yourself apart from the competition.

In Essence

- Conduct demographic and psychographic market research
- Understand the needs, desires, and behaviors of target audience
- Segment audience by developing specific Ideal Client Avatars
- Tailor products, services, and marketing efforts to reach different segments
- Continually reassess and update target audience profiles

What Did We Learn?

****True/False Questions:****

1. **True or False:** Neglecting to define the specific demographics and psychographics relevant to your target market will have minimal impact on your business success.

2. **True or False:** One of the consequences of not identifying your target market accurately is wasting valuable time and resources on the wrong audience.

3. **True or False:** Developing an Ideal Client Avatar can help entrepreneurs channel their resources more efficiently.

4. **True or False:** High customer acquisition costs are often a result of failing to understand who your ideal customers are.

****Multiple Choice Questions:****

1. **What is one of the biggest mistakes a small business owner can make regarding their market?**
   A. Overestimating their sales potential
   B. Neglecting to define specific demographics and psychographics
   C. Investing too heavily in online advertisements
   D. Hiring too many employees too quickly

2. **Monte realized his target audience was not:**
   A. Local teenagers
   B. Elderly scam victims
   C. High-end tech professionals
   D. Large corporations

3. **What was Monte's main lesson learned from his experience with scam victims?**
   A. Offering free services builds customer loyalty
   B. It's important to provide personalized tutorials
   C. Not all clients are worth the time and energy
   D. Expanding his services without research leads to growth

4. **What should be the first step in understanding your customer base?**
   A. Creating targeted marketing campaigns
   B. Conducting demographic and psychographic research
   C. Offering discounts based on customer feedback
   D. Developing a new product line

****Fill in the Blanks Questions:****

1. Without a clear understanding of who your ideal customers are, you won't be able to tailor your______ ________________ or _______________ to meet their specific needs.

1. High customer acquisition costs and low conversion rates are a direct result of _____________ to the wrong audience.

2. Monte used to get referrals mostly from ___________ clients who needed far more than just a quick fix.

3. The ultimate realization that dawned on Monte was that despite his best intentions, these scam victims were not his ______________.

Find the Answer Key in the Online Companion Members Area

As the previous chapter illustrated, neglecting to define specific demographics and psychographics can have detrimental effects on a company's marketing efforts. However, equally crucial is understanding your ideal client's pain points and needs from their perspective, which we will explore in the following chapter, as it is vital to successfully connect with and cater to your target audience. Keep reading to discover the importance of addressing these critical elements in your marketing strategy.

"Marketing Myth-stake"

How Ignoring Client Pain Points is Sabotaging Your Business Development

Your Ideal Client's Pain Points and Desires are Critical to Understand.

As an entrepreneur or small business owner, your success hinges on your ability to understand and cater to the needs and desires of your target audience. However, one common mistake that can sabotage your business development is overlooking the importance of understanding your ideal client's pain points and needs. This mistake can lead to missed opportunities, wasted resources, and ultimately, a failure to connect with and retain your customer base.

So why is overlooking the importance of understanding your ideal client's pain points and needs a mistake? Simply put, it is because these pain points and needs are the driving force behind consumer behavior. By understanding what motivates your ideal clients and what challenges they face, you can tailor your products or services to address those specific pain points, thereby increasing your appeal and relevance to them.

There are three main reasons why entrepreneurs and small business owners make the mistake of overlooking client pain points:

1. **Lack of Research:** Many entrepreneurs are so excited about their idea or product that they fail to conduct the correct market research to truly understand their target audience's pain points and needs.

2. **Assumption:** Some business owners make the mistake of assuming they already understand their ideal client's pain points, based on their own experiences or biases, without validating their assumptions through data and research.

3. **Focused on Features:** Instead of focusing on addressing client pain points, entrepreneurs may become too focused on promoting the features of their product or service, without considering how those features directly address their client's needs.

Entrepreneurs tend to make this mistake at the early stages of their business development, when they are still in the ideation or product development phase. However, this mistake can persist as the business grows and evolves, leading to missed opportunities for growth and a failure to truly connect with their target audience.

Consequences:
You think you understand your ideal client, but if you overlook their pain points and needs, you're in for a rude awakening. Not only will you struggle to connect with your audience, you will also miss out on crucial opportunities for growth.

You'll create products or services that won't truly resonate with your audience, leading to missed sales and lost revenue. Furthermore, your marketing efforts will fall flat, as you'll fail to address the core issues that drive your customers to seek out your solutions in the first place.

In short, the consequences of overlooking the importance of understanding your ideal client's pain points and needs are much worse than you think. It's not just about missing out on a few potential sales—it's about stunting the growth and success of your business in a fundamental way. Don't make the mistake of assuming you know your client's needs without truly understanding those needs from their own perspective.

The Best Way to Avoid, Fix, or Prevent Making This Mistake
The number one solution for the mistake of overlooking the importance of understanding your ideal client's pain points and needs is to utilize buyer behavior psychographics.

Using buyer behavior psychographics allows you to gain a deep understanding of your ideal client's desires, beliefs, values, and behavior, which in turn allows you to tailor your products or services to meet their specific needs.

The goal is to understand the specific behaviors, attitudes, and motivations of your target audience. By analyzing this data, you can gain valuable insight into what makes your ideal clients tick and tailor your marketing efforts accordingly.

Additionally, you can leverage social listening tools to monitor online conversations and gather feedback from your target audience in real time. This will allow you to stay informed about any changes in buyer behavior and adjust your strategies accordingly.

Another effective approach is to create buyer Avatars based on your research findings. This will help you visualize and understand the specific needs, pain points, and preferences of your ideal clients, enabling you to tailor your messaging and offerings to better resonate with them.

In the real world, companies like Nike have used buyer behavior psychographics to identify the specific lifestyles, attitudes, and values of their target audience, allowing them to create highly effective marketing campaigns and product offerings that resonate with their ideal clients.

Similarly, Airbnb has leveraged buyer behavior psychographics to better understand the motivations and preferences of their customers, allowing them to tailor their platform to meet the specific needs of different traveler segments.

Additionally, companies like Apple and Coca Cola have utilized social listening and market research to stay informed about changes in buyer behavior and adjust their marketing strategies in response, enabling them to stay at the forefront of their respective industries.

By following these examples and taking a proactive approach to understanding your ideal client's pain points and needs with buyer behavior psychographics, you can set your business up for sustained success and growth.

To put this into immediate action, start by conducting specific psychographic market research like surveys, interviews, and data analysis to identify patterns and trends in your ideal client's behavior and preferences. People love to talk about their obstacles and heartaches, which is a great way to identify those emotional hot topics. After you have some data collected, you can look for patterns, similarities, and their differences.

Once you have a solid understanding of your ideal client's psychographics, use this information to guide your marketing strategies, product development, and customer service approach.

Here are four practical examples of this in action in the real world:

1. A fitness apparel company uses buyer behavior psychographics to discover that their target audience **values sustainability and ethical production.** They adjust their manufacturing process to be more environmentally friendly, which resonates with their ideal clients and leads to increased sales.

2. A software company discovers through psychographics research that their ideal clients **prioritize ease of use and seamless integration with other platforms.** They use this information to update their user interface and improve compatibility with other software, resulting in higher customer satisfaction and retention.

3. A restaurant chain utilizes psychographics data to understand that their target audience **values convenience and healthy eating options.** They introduce a mobile ordering app and expand their menu to include more nutritious choices, which attracts new customers and increases loyalty among existing ones.

4. A consulting firm learns through psychographics analysis that their ideal clients **value innovation and forward-thinking strategies.** They use this insight to

rebrand their services as cutting-edge and futuristic, attracting clients who are eager to embrace new ideas and approaches.

By leveraging buyer behavior psychographics, entrepreneurs and small business owners can gain a competitive edge by truly understanding and addressing the needs and pain points of their ideal clients.

Helpful Resources

- **The Ideal Client Map online companion members area** – Chapter 5
  - Access Resources here: https://resources.theidealclientmap.com
  - Where to plug emotional pain points into TICM

- **TICM Online Training:** The Ideal Client Map Online Training is a visual tool and training that helps you 'see' the emotional relationships of your Ideal Client Avatar.
  - Without a visual tool it takes a ton of brain power to keep all the pain points and emotional thoughts on track.
  - Stop using words to keep track of emotions and the emotional triggers.
  - Start using visuals to make it easy.

Monte's Top Piece of Advice

Here's my biggest piece of advice when it comes to the importance of understanding your ideal client's pain points and needs: Take extra time to accurately map out the specific and relevant pain points of your Ideal Client Avatar.

To effectively market (and sell) to your ideal client, you need to know what makes them tick and what they are saying in their own heads about their own pain. By understanding this specific psychographic, you can tailor your messaging and offerings to truly resonate with them on a deeper level.

Monte's Story of Steven's Struggle and How TICM Was Born:
It all started during a pivotal moment in my entrepreneurial journey. I was retiring the computer repair side of my business, and as one chapter closed, another remarkable chapter began. My friend Steven, a brilliant yet struggling entrepreneur, was trying to navigate the labyrinthine world of creating and marketing his new course. His enthusiasm was palpable, and his dedication unquestionable, but he was caught in a web of confusion and frustration.

Steven had diligently filled in his Ideal Client Avatar (ICA) data points, hoping to use them as a North Star for his entire process. He thought he had it all figured out: the wants, pains, problems, questions, objections, and ultimate results of his ideal clients. Yet, something was missing. As we pieced together all the individual elements of his course and sales page, it became apparent to me that while we had assembled all the parts, the whole was less than the sum of these parts.

The issue was clear: there was a lack of congruency. Something in Steven's ICA didn't quite sit right, but explaining this to him was a different story altogether. Despite my best efforts to articulate what I was seeing, Steven remained bewildered. Our conversations began to feel like we were speaking two different languages, and no matter how much I pointed out the discrepancies on his Avatar form, he couldn't see what I was seeing.

Steven's persistence was admirable. He tried countless combinations, mixing and matching elements in an attempt to find the elusive key that would unlock the coherence and effectiveness he needed. Over and over, he went through the motions—yet, the underlying alignment of his ICA remained elusive. Each combination felt like an isolated tactic rather than part of a seamless strategy. It was painful to witness; his efforts were not addressing the true problem.

As I watched Steven struggle, a thought crystallized in my mind: "There must be a better way to show Steven this pattern I can see." It was a eureka moment, the kind that sends shivers down your spine, and I knew I had to find a way to visualize what words could not convey. That's when I conceived the idea of creating a mind map—but not just any mind map. This would be different, something that Steven had never seen before.

I crafted The Ideal Client Map (TICM) with meticulous care. It wasn't the conventional mind map filled with disjointed bulleted lists. Instead, I designed an actual map of a thought journey, with interconnected nodes representing different facets of the client's path, linked not just linearly but in a multidimensional manner. It was an intricate depiction of a single train of thought, flowing smoothly from one point to the next, capturing the essence of a client's thinking in a way that was as intuitive as it was insightful.

When I showed Steven this new kind of mind map, the impact was immediate. His face lit up with understanding as he followed the tracks I had laid out. For the first time, he could see how to tie his Avatar's wants, pains, problems, questions, objections, and ultimate results together in a cohesive and meaningful way. It was like seeing the scattered pieces of a puzzle finally click into place.

Once Steven embraced the power of The Ideal Client Map, it was transformative. He corrected his course, refined his copy, and revamped his marketing plan. The shifts he made brought a seamless flow to his processes that had previously been fragmented and disjointed. The clarity and coherence that TICM provided were nothing short of revolutionary for Steven's business.

Steven didn't just stop at improving his current project. He began to use The Ideal Client Map for all his business decisions. He found that this approach saved him a tremendous amount of brainpower and time. By visualizing the interconnectedness of his clients' thoughts and needs, he could make decisions with confidence and precision. I saw Steven blossom into a more strategic and effective entrepreneur right before my eyes.

Inspired by Steven's success, I expanded TICM and created supplemental trainings to further support and amplify the process. Just like any great invention, The Ideal Client Map had a journey of its own, evolving and refining as I gathered more insights and experiences. Each step of this journey provided new learnings that contributed to the growing utility and applicability of TICM.

Now, as Steven continues to streamline his business, I, too, revel in the ongoing journey of discovery with The Ideal Client Map. Every day brings new experiences and insights, fuelling the continuous growth of TICM. It is not just a tool; it's a dynamic framework that evolves with every challenge and triumph we encounter.

In retrospect, helping Steven understand his Ideal Client Avatar better by mind mapping their 'trains of thought' didn't just transform his business; it transformed mine as well. The Ideal Client Map is now a critical part of my toolkit, a beacon that guides entrepreneurs toward greater clarity and congruency in their marketing strategies. And the journey, I am thrilled to say, is far from over.

This is crucial because it allows you to create products and services that address their specific pain points and needs, making your business more appealing and relevant to them. It also helps you craft marketing messages that speak directly to their desires and motivations, increasing the likelihood that they will connect with your brand and become a loyal customer.

Now that you understand the importance of buyer behavior psychographics when understanding your ideal client, you can get started by conducting the right research and gathering the relevant data on your target audience. Use this information to map out your Avatar, refine your marketing plan, and watch as you attract and retain more qualified customers.

Chapter Summary

- Understand buyer behavior psychographics
- Tailor products/services to meet specific needs
- Don't assume you know what customers want
- Set your business up for success with research and understanding your ICA's psychographics
- Map out your ICA's train of thought visually

What Did We Learn?

****True/False Questions:****

1. **True or False:** Overlooking the importance of understanding your ideal client's pain points and needs does not significantly impact your business growth.

2. **True or False:** Conducting thorough market research can help identify the pain points and needs of your target audience.

3. **True or False:** Business owners who focus solely on the features of their product without considering client needs are likely to miss opportunities.

4. **True or False:** Social listening tools are ineffective in gathering real-time feedback from your target audience.

****Multiple Choice Questions:****

1. **What is a common mistake entrepreneurs make regarding their ideal client's pain points and needs?**
   A. Conducting too much research
   B. Assuming they understand their client's pain points without validation
   C. Focusing solely on their competitor's strategies
   D. Over-investing in client feedback

2. **Which of the following is NOT a reason why entrepreneurs overlook client pain points?**
   A. Lack of research
   B. Assumption based on biases
   C. Overemphasis on product features
   D. Constantly updating their product based on client feedback

3. **How can buyer behavior psychographics help your business?**
   A. By increasing product prices
   B. By understanding your competition's strengths
   C. By gaining deep insights into your client's desires, beliefs, values, and behavior
   D. By enhancing your office décor

4. **Which company is mentioned as using buyer behavior psychographics successfully?**
   A. Microsoft
   B. Nike
   C. Google
   D. Tesla

****Fill in the Blanks Questions:****

1. One consequence of not understanding your client's pain points is that your marketing efforts will ________________.

2. Companies like ____________ and Coca Cola have utilized social listening and market research to stay informed about changes in buyer behavior.

3. The process of creating ________________ based on research findings can help visualize the specific needs and preferences of ideal clients.

4. By _____________ buyer behavior psychographics, businesses can tailor their products and services to better resonate with their target audience.

Find the Answer Key in the Online Companion Members Area

To truly connect with your ideal client, you'll need to understand their pain points and perspectives. However, this is just the first step in building strong relationships - the next chapter will explore the equally critical mistake of underestimating the importance of building emotional connections with your ideal client, a crucial element in fostering lasting and meaningful client relationships. Keep reading to learn how to avoid this common pitfall and create deeper connections with your clients.

"Beyond Transactions"

Underestimating the Value of Emotional Connection in Your Business Development

Building Emotional Connections with Your Ideal Client is Smart.

When it comes to building a successful business, many entrepreneurs and small business owners focus solely on the transactional side of things. They are so busy trying to sell their products or services that they underestimate the importance of building emotional connections with their ideal clients. This is a huge mistake that can ultimately hinder their business growth and success.

This is a big mistake because it disregards the fact that emotional connections lead to long-lasting and loyal relationships. When clients feel emotionally connected to a business, they are more likely to become repeat customers and refer the business to others. This can ultimately lead to increased revenue and business growth.

Entrepreneurs and small business owners often make the mistake of underestimating the importance of building emotional connections with their ideal clients for several reasons.

1. **Lack of Time:** Most seem to be caught up in the day-to-day operations of their business and fail to prioritize client relationships.

2. **Focus on Products:** Many may believe that their product or service alone is enough to attract and retain clients, without recognizing the value of emotional connections.

3. **Lack of Knowledge:** Some business owners may simply lack the knowledge or understanding of how to effectively build and maintain emotional connections with their clients.

This mistake tends to be made when entrepreneurs and small business owners are in the early stages of their business or when they are facing challenges or competition in the market. During these times, they may be solely focused on making sales and generating revenue, overlooking the long-term benefits of emotional connections with clients.

Consequences:
The consequences of underestimating the importance of building emotional connections with your ideal client are long term and compounding.

Firstly, you will lose out on repeat business and referrals. Your clients will not feel loyal to you or compelled to recommend your business to others if they don't feel emotionally connected to your brand.

Secondly, your business will struggle to stand out in a crowded market. Without emotional connections, your brand will blend in with the competition, making it difficult to capture your ideal client's attention and loyalty.

Lastly, you will miss out on vital feedback only available from emotionally connected customers. Without these connected customers, your feedback will lack **the most helpful** suggestions, comments, and concerns.

These consequences are much worse than you might think because emotional connections are essential for long-term success. Without them, your business will fail to thrive and expand, putting your livelihood and financial stability at risk.

In conclusion, underestimating the importance of building emotional connections with your ideal client can lead to a dramatic decline in business success and potential financial ruin. It's crucial to prioritize emotional connections in order to build a sustainable, loyal client base and create a thriving, prosperous business.

Typical Scenarios

Many entrepreneurs and small business owners try using personalized email campaigns, scheduling one-on-one interview meetings, or even hosting generic client appreciation events. However, these solutions don't work very well because they still lack emotional connection too.

Clients can see right through these attempts and may feel even more disconnected as a result. Everyone can tell when they receive an email from an autoresponder. No one likes meetings, and particularly if they are going to be drilled with questions. And a BBQ is nice, but if you cater to introverts then this isn't the best way to connect with them.

Building genuine emotional connections takes time and authentic effort, and simply going through the motions of personal interactions without truly caring about the client will not lead to meaningful connections. Instead of simply going through the motions, it's crucial for entrepreneurs to genuinely understand their clients' needs, show empathy, and act with authenticity in order to build strong emotional connections.

The Best Way to Avoid, Fix, or Prevent Making This Mistake
Avoid underestimating the importance of building emotional connections with your ideal client by creating personalized connections with them.

This works like magic because emotional connections lead to loyalty, trust, and long-term relationships with your clients. When your clients feel understood, valued, and appreciated on a personal level, they are more likely to remain loyal to your brand and refer others to you.

One great way to avoid underestimating the importance of building emotional connections with your ideal client is to prioritize personal connections with your clients. This means taking the time to understand their needs, concerns, and aspirations on a deeper level. By doing so, you can create a stronger bond with your clients and gain important insights that will help you better serve them.

Start by getting to know your ideal client on a deeper level. Find out their likes, dislikes, challenges, and goals. Show genuine interest in their lives and try to connect with them on a personal level.

Here are four practical examples of this solution in action:

1. Plan a client appreciation event that caters specifically to your best clients. Provide the right entertainment, amenities, and **the things your clients value the most.**

2. Send personalized thank-you notes or strategic gifts to show your clients that you value them as individuals. What is a strategic gift? Simply put, it is **a well thought out gift that addresses a specific and relevant need or desire of the recipient.**

3. Use social media to engage with your clients on a personal level by commenting on their posts and sharing their successes. Sharing relevant things posted by your clients shows them how much you care. Additionally, **giving a 'wow' or 'love' is much more powerful than a simple 'like'.**

4. Implement a relevant client loyalty program that rewards clients for their continued support and loyalty to your business. Notice a 'relevant' theme going on here? Giving a gift simply for the joy of giving is a great way for friends and family to share and connect on an emotional level. When it comes to your clients, a **relevant gift that provides value** is more likely to make that emotional connection because they now have a strong reason to connect the gift to you.

Remember to engage in meaningful conversations, show genuine interest in their lives, and express empathy towards their challenges. This not only fosters trust and loyalty, but it also sets you apart from competitors who may not prioritize emotional connections.

Building emotional connections with your clients is not just a one-time effort, but an ongoing process that requires genuine care and attention.

By creating personal connections with your clients, you will build strong relationships that lead to long-term success for your business.

Helpful Resources:

- **The Ideal Client Map online companion members area** – Chapter 6
  - Access Resources here: https://resources.theidealclientmap.com

- Where to put emotional connections into TICM
- Practically Perfect Priority Pyramid
- Helps you identify priorities based on perspective

- **Use DISC communication styles to amplify your messages**:
  - Read "The Secret Sales Code: Skyrocket Clicks, Sales, and Conversions Using DISC Communication Styles in Your Sales Copywriting and Content Marketing" by Jim Edwards
  - https://www.amazon.com/Secret-Sales-Code-Conversions-Communication-ebook/dp/B0CGY25VYK/

- The Ideal Client Map Training:
  - **The Thought Process Bonus Training** helps you get inside your Avatar's head so you can 'see' what they are thinking. http://mapyouridealclient.com

Monte's Top Tip

Here's my biggest advice on this issue:
"Start with developing an emotionally accurate Ideal Client Avatar for your most desired and sought after client."

As an entrepreneur or small business owner, it can be easy to focus solely on the product or service you are offering, but it is essential to remember that at the heart of every successful business is a strong emotional connection with your customers.

Building emotional connections with your ideal client is crucial because it creates a sense of trust, loyalty, and understanding. When customers feel an emotional connection to your brand, they are more likely to become repeat customers and recommend your business to others. In today's competitive market, where customers have endless options, the emotional bond they have with a brand can be the deciding factor in their purchasing decisions.

"Let me take you back a few years to when I first met Leonard."

Leonard wasn't just any client; he was one of those customers who others might describe as challenging, demanding, and precise. He knew exactly what he wanted and expected nothing short of perfection. Some folks found it downright daunting to work with him. But to me, Leonard was an opportunity. An opportunity to understand someone deeply and meet their exact needs.

You see, Leonard had been a long-term client of my local computer service and repair business. I made it my mission to understand what made him tick and why he liked what he did. Most people couldn't comprehend his level of specificity, but I saw it as a puzzle waiting to be solved. By learning about his personal desires and motivations, I was able to craft custom solutions that worked for him, not just from a technical standpoint, but from his perspective.

Every time Leonard contacted me, I made it a point to listen to him intently, grasp his concerns, and provide solutions that matched his requirements to a T. This earned me his trust and gratitude, and soon enough, he began relying on me for all his technological needs. But then came a challenge that tested our rapport like never before.

Leonard had to adapt to some new technology for his work. He purchased high-end equipment that promised simplicity and efficiency. But instead of seamless integration, he hit a wall. Despite following the instructions meticulously, he kept running into the same error. Hours of Googling turned up nothing. Frustrated, Leonard walked into my office, his equipment in tow.

After some initial troubleshooting, I managed to get the equipment up and running. But this wasn't how Leonard envisioned things. The process to operate the equipment was convoluted and far from user-friendly. Worse, manipulating the video files was a nightmare, requiring a series of steps that even a tech-savvy individual would find overwhelming. Leonard was upset, feeling deceived by the promise of simplicity that the equipment's marketing had boasted.

I knew I had to put myself in Leonard’s shoes. Diagnosing the situation from his perspective, I identified exactly what he wanted: a straightforward, logical process that met his specific needs without the hassle. I wasn't just fixing a technical issue; I was solving a human problem. After thorough research, I found an alternative set of equipment that perfectly aligned with Leonard's expectations.

The best part? He could return that complex system and purchase the new, user-friendly equipment at a considerable saving. The new system was intuitive enough that Leonard managed to set it up all by himself. It was a win-win solution that brought a smile to his face and reaffirmed his trust in me.

From that moment on, Leonard never made another technology-related decision without consulting me first. But it didn't stop there. He started recommending my services to everyone he knew. Friends, colleagues, even casual acquaintances – if they needed tech advice, Leonard would insist they call me before making any purchases.

My approach to understanding Leonard and addressing his needs created an emotional connection that went beyond mere client satisfaction. It built a level of trust that not only ensured repeat business from Leonard but also turned him into a powerful advocate for my services. The ripple effect of empathy and personalized service led to a host of new clients who valued and were willing to pay for my expertise.

By truly understanding Leonard's needs and addressing them from his point of view, I managed to turn a potentially difficult customer into one of my greatest assets. It's a testament to the power of emotional connections in business – when you genuinely care about your clients and see the world through their eyes, you create bonds that go beyond transactions. And those are the relationships that truly stand the test of time.

Now that you better understand the importance of building emotional connections with your ideal client, I encourage you to take action on what you've learned in this chapter.

Start by getting to know your customers on a more personal level, understanding their specific needs, desires, and pain point perspectives. Use this insight to tailor your marketing strategies and customer experiences to resonate with them emotionally. By doing so, you will not only build stronger connections with your customers but also set your business apart in the market.

Chapter Summary

- Prioritize personal connections with clients
- Understand their needs, concerns, and aspirations on a deeper level
- Engage in meaningful conversations and show genuine interest
- Express empathy towards their challenges
- Building emotional connections is an ongoing process requiring genuine care and attention

What Did We Learn?

****True/False Questions:****

1. **True/False:** Entrepreneurs should prioritize building emotional connections with clients over making sales.

2. **True/False:** Personal interactions, even if they lack authenticity, are sufficient to build strong emotional connections with clients.

3. **True/False:** Building emotional connections can lead to increased customer loyalty and referrals.

4. **True/False:** Emotional connections with clients are primarily beneficial in the early stages of a business.

****Multiple Choice Questions:****

1. **Why do many entrepreneurs fail to build emotional connections with their clients?**
   A. Due to lack of time
   B. Believing that products alone will attract clients
   C. Lack of knowledge
   D. All of the above

2. **What is a consequence of not building emotional connections with clients?**
   A. Increased competition
   B. Higher operational costs
   C. Losing out on repeat business and referrals
   D. Improved client feedback

3. **Which method is NOT effective in creating genuine emotional connections?**
   A. Personalized email campaigns
   B. Scheduling one-on-one interview meetings
   C. Hosting generic client appreciation events
   D. Engaging in meaningful conversations

4. **What is the ultimate benefit of building emotional connections with your clients?**
   A. Immediate financial gain
   B. Short-term operational success
   C. Long-term client loyalty and business growth
   D. Reduced marketing efforts

****Fill-in-the-Blanks Questions:****

1. Building genuine emotional connections requires time and ____________.

2. When clients feel ________________, valued, and appreciated, they are more likely to remain loyal to your brand.

3. One way to build emotional connections is by understanding your clients' needs, concerns, and ________________.

4. Emotional connections foster trust and _______, setting your business apart from competitors.

Find the Answer Key in the Online Companion Members Area

As our previous chapter highlighted, underestimating the importance of building emotional connections with ideal clients can prove detrimental to business growth. However, equally damaging is the mistake of not gathering feedback from existing clients to continuously enhance our ideal client profile. Let's explore the impact of this oversight and the opportunities it presents for improvement. Keep reading to discover how this essential feedback can streamline your marketing approach and strengthen your client relationships.

"The Forgetful Flaw"

Why Existing Clients' Feedback Matters

Don't Forget to Gather Feedback from Your Own Existing Clients.

As we have been discussing in each chapter, understanding your ideal client avatar is crucial for the success of your business. It guides your marketing efforts, product development, and overall business strategy.

However, a huge mistake that many entrepreneurs make is not gathering feedback from existing clients to enhance their ideal client avatar. This forgetful flaw is like leaving money just sitting there on the table.

What exactly do I mean by leaving money on the table?

1. **Your existing clients are a gold mine of information about your target audience.** They have already purchased your products or services and have direct experience with your business. Their feedback is invaluable in understanding what attracts them to your business and what could be improved to better cater to their needs. Even if they are not your ideal client!

2. **You're missing opportunities for improvement and growth.** Without a clear understanding of your existing clients' experiences with your brand, you

may be missing out on valuable insights that could help you better serve your target audience and attract new clients.

3. **You could be spending money and effort on the wrong things.** You're risking a disconnect between what you think your ideal client avatar needs and what they actually want. By specifically asking them, you can identify the things they want, instead of trying to convince them of the things you think they need.

This mistake is most commonly made when people are focused on acquiring new clients and expanding their customer base but can happen at any point in the entrepreneurial journey. While acquiring new clients is important for business growth, neglecting existing clients can be detrimental to the long-term success of your business. Additionally, some entrepreneurs may assume that they already have a clear understanding of their ideal client avatar and overlook the importance of gathering ongoing feedback from existing clients.

Consequences:
Not gathering feedback from your existing clients causes some severe setbacks. You are essentially operating in the dark. Without understanding the needs and preferences of your current clients, you risk attracting the wrong audience and missing out on potential business opportunities. This

mistake can lead to a decline in sales, a damaged reputation, burnout, and even the failure of your business.

Even if your current clients are not your ideal clients, you can gain valuable information from them. What attracted them to you? What do they find valuable from your services? What would entice them to continue doing business with you? Yes, the answers to these questions can help you find your ideal client because they provide you with information on what NOT to do.

In conclusion, not gathering feedback from your own existing clients, ideal or not, is like leaving money on the table because that extremely valuable and super relevant market research data is FREE!

The Best Way to Avoid, Fix, or Prevent Making This Mistake
I'm sure you guessed it by now. Actively seeking customer feedback and reviews is the best option to gain valuable insights into the needs, preferences, and pain points of your existing clients. In turn, this will help you refine your Ideal Client Avatar and better tailor your products or services to meet their needs.

How does one go about obtaining the right kind of customer feedback?
Start by reaching out to your existing clients and asking through surveys, interviews, or simply through direct communication. If they are a completely happy customer, encourage them to leave reviews on platforms such as

Google, Yelp, or social media. If they have suggestions, recommendations, or even complaints, then ask them to contact you directly so you can personally address them.

Here are four detailed, practical examples of how this solution works in the real world:

1. A small business owner in the health and wellness industry **actively seeks feedback from their existing clients through surveys and interviews**. They discover that their Ideal Client Avatar is primarily interested in holistic healing and stress-relief techniques, prompting them to adjust their services and marketing to better cater to these needs.

2. An entrepreneur running a digital marketing agency **encourages their clients to leave reviews on Google and LinkedIn**. By analyzing these reviews, they identify common pain points and concerns among their ideal clients, allowing them to adjust their service offerings and messaging to better address these issues.

3. A startup founder in the e-commerce space regularly **gathers feedback from their existing customers through email surveys and social media polls**. Through this feedback, they realize that their ideal clients are primarily interested in eco-friendly

and sustainable products, prompting them to adjust their product offerings and marketing messaging accordingly.

4. A consultant for small businesses actively **seeks feedback from their clients through one-on-one conversations and feedback forms**. By listening to their clients' needs and concerns, they are able to refine their ideal client avatar and tailor their services to better meet the unique needs of their target audience.

In practice, successful companies like Airbnb have used customer feedback to improve their services. By listening to their customers and making necessary adjustments, they have managed to attract a larger customer base. Another example is Amazon, which constantly gathers feedback and reviews to enhance their products and user experience. Similarly, companies like Zappos and Apple rely on customer feedback to continuously improve their offerings and better serve their target audience. By prioritizing customer feedback and reviews, these businesses have been able to stay competitive and relevant in their industries.

If you're an entrepreneur or small business owner who hasn't gathered feedback from existing clients to enhance your ideal client avatar, don't worry. It's not too late to fix this mistake. Start by reaching out to your current clients and ask for their feedback. Make it a priority to regularly engage with your clients and ask for their honest opinions about your products or services.

You can also check your online reviews to understand what your clients like and dislike about your products or services. Positive customer reviews can serve as powerful social proof and help attract new clients to your business. Additionally, negative reviews can be opportunities to engage with your audience and show them how much you care.

Embrace feedback as a tool for growth and improvement and use it to continuously refine and optimize your ideal client avatar. By investing this extra time and effort, you can refine your Ideal Client Avatar and make it even more accurate.

Helpful Resources:

- **Use an Email Responder to create questionnaires and feedback forms**
    - ➢ 'Gamify' when possible: quizzes, scavenger hunts, prizes
    - ➢ Monte's Pick: AWeber
    - ➢ https://montearmstrong.aweber.com/

- **The Ideal Client Map online companion members area** – Chapter 7
    - ➢ Access Resources here: https://resources.theidealclientmap.com

- The easy button to creating quizzes and workbooks

Monte's Experienced Advice

Here you go, my biggest advice on this issue:
"Don't forget about gathering feedback from your existing clients to better guide your business decisions!"

By seeking feedback from your current customers, you can gain valuable insight into their needs, preferences, and pain points. This information is crucial for refining your ideal client avatar and targeting your marketing efforts more effectively. Without this feedback, you may miss out on opportunities to better serve your clients and attract new ones.

Conversely, without this feedback, you may spend resources developing and offering services that your clients don't need or want.

"How Client Feedback Would Have Saved Me Hundreds of Dollars"

Running a successful local computer service and support business has required dedication, expertise, and an appetite for learning from my mistakes. I've cultivated a solid reputation for delivering reliable tech support and innovative solutions to my clients. However, not all my ideas have been that well-received. In a previous chapter of my entrepreneurial journey, I spent considerable time, energy, and money developing a new service for my existing customers, only to realize that I had missed one crucial step: getting customer feedback.

The concept seemed brilliant at the onset. I thought I would enhance my service list by offering video ads for social media. Leveraging the power of visual content on platforms like Facebook and Instagram appeared to be a game-changer. After all, video marketing is widely praised for its effectiveness in drawing attention and driving engagement. I confidently assumed my current clients would see the value and jump at the opportunity. With this vision in mind, I invested in high-quality video editing software, took relevant courses on video marketing, and set up a streamlined process for creating captivating video ads.

When it came time to pitch this new service, I was optimistic. I started with the businesses I had strong relationships with: local restaurants, auto repair shops, and property management companies. I thought these industries, in particular, could benefit from the enhanced visibility that social media videos could provide. However, instead of the enthusiastic reception I anticipated, I was met with a wall of polite but firm rejections. Each business I approached declined my offer, leaving me puzzled and increasingly frustrated.

As odd as it may sound, these business owners were simply not interested in attracting more attention on social media through video ads.

They had their own reasons; they maintained that their current customer base was sufficient, or they believed their clientele didn't rely on social media for information. Despite my best efforts to enlighten them about the untapped potential of this approach, the feedback was unanimous. They didn't share my vision.

I vividly remember one particular incident that stands as the climax of this ill-fated endeavor. Determined to convert one of my most loyal clients into hiring me to create a video social media post, I pushed forward relentlessly. My intention was to offer them an immensely beneficial service, but my execution left much to be desired. As I tried to sell them on the idea, I saw a shift in their demeanor. They became annoyed and frustrated, and it struck me that I was wasting their valuable time. They didn't need another sales pitch—they needed a solution to a problem I hadn't recognized.

Realizing the gravity of the situation, I paused and did something I should have done from the beginning: I listened. They made it clear that they didn't want the benefits I was describing. They had specific needs that my new service wasn't addressing. They told me bluntly that I was 'barking up the wrong tree.' In seeking to help them, I had failed to grasp what they actually required.

In a moment of candid revelation, my client articulated what they truly needed: an easier way to display updated business hours on their website. This was a straightforward, immediate problem affecting their day-to-day operations. Against the backdrop of my complex video ad pitch, this simple solution was a eureka moment. I knew I could deliver this functionality swiftly and effectively.

We collaborated to set up a website widget that, when installed, would automatically display their most recent Facebook post. This way, they could update their hours easily by posting directly to Facebook, a social media platform they were already comfortable with. There was no need for them to learn how to manage their website's backend or reach out to me each time they needed an update. It was a practical, easy-to-implement solution that perfectly met their needs.

The relief and appreciation from my client were palpable. This experience taught me an invaluable lesson: if only I had asked my clients beforehand what they truly needed, I could have directed my efforts towards solving their actual problems rather than projecting my assumptions onto them. I had spent hundreds of dollars and countless hours developing a service no one asked for, and the solution they needed was something I was well-equipped to provide all along.

Effective entrepreneurship is not just about having great ideas; it's about ensuring those ideas align with the needs of your customers. This experience underscored the critical importance of customer feedback in developing new services. By actively listening and engaging with my clients, I can continue to grow my business in ways that truly benefit those I aim to serve.

It's important to consistently gather and analyze customer feedback to stay ahead of the curve and ensure that your business continues to meet the needs of your target audience. By taking action on the feedback received, you can improve your products or services, enhance the customer experience, and ultimately drive growth and success for your business.

In conclusion, make it a priority to gather feedback from your existing clients and use it to enhance your ideal client avatar. This practice will help you better understand and serve your target audience, leading to increased customer satisfaction and business growth.

Chapter Summary

- Actively seek feedback and reviews from existing clients
- Regularly engage with clients and ask for their honest opinions
- Use feedback to refine ideal client avatar and tailor offerings

- Positive customer reviews can serve as powerful social proof
- Embrace feedback as a tool for growth and improvement

What Did We Learn?
****True/False Questions:****

1. **True/False:** Gathering feedback from existing clients is less important than acquiring new clients.

2. **True/False:** Failing to gather feedback from current clients means you're likely missing out on vital information.

3. **True/False:** Existing clients' feedback is irrelevant if they are not your ideal clients.

4. **True/False:** Customer reviews help in refining your Ideal Client Avatar through direct experiences.

****Multiple Choice Questions:****

1. **What is one major benefit of gathering feedback from existing clients?**
   A. It helps you employ more staff
   B. It provides invaluable insights into what attracts them to your business
   C. It decreases workload
   D. It reduces marketing costs

2. **What methods did successful companies, such as Airbnb and Amazon, use to improve their services?**
   A. Guesswork
   B. Market trends
   C. Customer feedback
   D. Competitor analysis

3. **Which platform can happy customers use to leave reviews for your business?**
   A. Google
   B. Yelp
   C. Social Media
   D. All of the above

4. **Why is it a mistake to focus solely on acquiring new clients?**
   A. It can lead to a high rate of client turnover
   B. It shows a lack of ambition
   C. You risk neglecting existing clients' feedback
   D. It's expensive

****Fill-in-the-Blanks Questions:****

1. ________________ from existing clients can help you better cater to your target audience's needs.

2. Suitable ways to gather feedback include customer surveys, interviews, and ________________.

3. Businesses that prioritize customer feedback, such as ______________ and ______________, remain competitive in their industries.

4. Feedback is not just about gathering opinions but can also serve as a ________________ for growth and improvement.

Find the Answer Key in the Online Companion Members Area

In failing to gather feedback from existing clients to refine their ideal client avatar, businesses miss out on valuable insights that could inform their target audience strategies. This oversight often leads to a reliance on intuition rather than data to define their audience, a mistake that can significantly impact the effectiveness of their marketing efforts. Keep reading to discover the risks of making decisions based on assumptions rather than concrete information.

"The Confidence Trap"

Overestimating Your Knowledge of Your Target Audience

Intuition Without Data is not Enough to Understand Your Target Audience

It's easy to fall into the trap of relying on intuition rather than data to define our target audience. We may have a certain level of confidence in our understanding of who our customers are, but this confidence can be misleading.

In reality, relying on intuition can lead to inaccurate client profiles because our biases, assumptions, and limited experiences can unknowingly cloud our judgment and lead us to make incorrect assumptions about our target audience. This can result in your business targeting the wrong people or using ineffective marketing strategies.

Relying on intuition rather than data can adversely impact your small business in several key areas:

1. It leads to making assumptions about your target audience without solid data to back them up.

2. A lack of concrete understanding can result in ineffective marketing strategies, wasted resources, and missed opportunities to connect with potential customers.

3. You're navigating in the dark and relying solely on guesswork to reach your audience.

This mistake is particularly troublesome because it limits your ability to fully understand the needs, desires, and pain points of your target audience. Without a deep understanding of who your ideal client is, it's impossible to develop a branding voice that resonates with them. More importantly, relying solely on intuition can lead you to make decisions that are disconnected from actual market realities. This detachment can pave the way for missed opportunities and heighten the risk of potential failure.

Entrepreneurs and small business owners make this mistake for the following reasons:

1. It's easy to think we know our target audience well because a version of ourselves is often our first customer. This can lead to a false sense of confidence in understanding our ideal clients.

2. There's often a lack of resources or time to conduct thorough market research, leading us to rely on our gut instincts rather than hard data.

3. The sheer prospect of market research can feel overwhelming and confusing to figure out where to start, adding another layer of reluctance to undertake this essential task.

This mistake is common in the early stages of business development when entrepreneurs and small business owners are eager to launch their products or services quickly leading them to do one of three things:

1. Get caught up in ideas and assumptions about who their customers truly are.

2. Assert what they would do if they were in their target audience's shoes.

3. Skip the step of conducting thorough market research and rely on their gut instincts.

While your target audience may share similar characteristics with you, market research will reveal nuanced information that could negate your assumptions.

Consequences:
Take a moment to consider the numerous consequences that stem from making assumptions and assertions about the living breathing humans you aim to serve. Wrong assumptions can lead you to waste time and resources on ineffective tactics that fail to address your target audience's genuine needs and desires. Without the right data to shape your strategies, the risk of launching products or services that fall flat in the market escalates exponentially, often leading to an erratic cycle of high and low sales.

Imagine striving to build a business on intuition alone. Many entrepreneurs are shackled by the belief that their gut feeling and can be a substitution for hard data, leading to a precarious over-reliance on intuition. There's no doubt intuition can be a valuable guide in some instances. However, intuition alone lacks the precision needed to decipher the multifaceted and evolving preferences that define your target audience.

Let Me (Anza) Tell You a Story About a Time I Didn't Understand My Ideal Client

My first Facebook ad campaign failed at epic proportions, costing me more than $10K. Yes, you heard that right—ten thousand dollars gone, and not a single ideal client in sight. It was the end of the year 2016, and I was a newly minted coach, brimming with enthusiasm and passion. I had just acquired a new set of skills and couldn't wait to share them with the world.

My plan?

To host a transformative retreat on a stunning tropical island, a haven where my future clients could rejuvenate and rediscover themselves. Weeks of meticulous planning, sleepless nights, and a significant amount of my savings went into preparing for this launch. I even hired a reputable marketing agency that specialized in coaches to help me build the perfect sales page and create eye-catching Facebook ad campaigns.

With Black Friday looming, my excitement was palpable. This was the ideal time to roll out my offer; potential clients could buy the retreat as a Christmas gift for themselves or their loved ones. We were racing against the clock, fine-tuning the ads, making sure every little detail was perfect before going live. The anticipation of starting this new chapter in my career was almost unbearable. I envisioned waking up to an inbox brimming with inquiries from eager clients, all ready to embark on this life-changing journey with me.

But reality had other plans. On Black Friday, I eagerly opened my email, heart pounding with excitement, only to be met with utter disappointment. My inbox was full, but the people reaching out were far from my ideal clients. They were mostly curious onlookers with no genuine interest in the retreat I had so passionately crafted. My heart sank, and a sense of devastation took over.

What went wrong?

We followed the script, checking all of the right demographics boxes inside Facebook's ad manager: age, gender, location, interests, and income. But we had overlooked something crucial—buying motivations and specific pain points. Our message lacked the depth and precision needed to resonate with the people I was genuinely meant to serve. The agency had painted with broad strokes, but they missed the fine details that make a message truly compelling. This experience was a bitter pill to swallow, but it was also an invaluable lesson!

To craft an ad that truly resonates, you need to dig deeper than mere demographics. You must understand the intricate layers of your audience's psyche: their likes, dislikes, lifestyle choices, and most importantly, how they perceive themselves versus the person they aspire to become. The copy needs to address these subtleties to bridge the gap between their current state and their desired future. It's about speaking directly to their hearts and minds, not just their wallets.

I realized that my approach had been fundamentally flawed. In my eagerness to launch quickly, my intuition led me to combine traits from various "ideal" clients, creating a hybrid, a super-client avatar. Instead of focusing on a specific, well-defined persona, I tried to appeal to *everyone* simultaneously. This muddled my message, making it too broad and diluted to impact anyone deeply. I was casting a wide net but catching nothing of value.

As I have since learned, effective copywriting is an art of precision. It requires an intimate understanding of a single archetype that is representative of your ideal client. This archetype has details so vivid that you can picture them reading your ad and thinking, "This is me." Only then can your message truly hit home, creating a bond of trust and interest that eventually leads to conversion. When you speak to everyone, you essentially speak to no one.

Remember, behind every successful ad is a compelling story that speaks directly to your target audience's soul. It's not just about the product or service you offer; it's about the transformation you promise. By learning this the hard way, I emerged better equipped to understand the power of a well-told story in copywriting. My loss wasn't just a financial setback but a stepping stone toward mastering the delicate balance between persuasive messaging and building genuine, trust-filled relationships.

So, if you're planning to launch a campaign anytime soon, learn from my costly mistake, and take a moment to observe your ideal client's world. Make it your goal to understand them better than they understand themselves. Speak directly to their hearts and watch as your efforts go from mediocre marketing campaigns to laser-focused strategies that resonate and deliver the results you worked so hard for. My devastating failure paved the way for future success, and I hope it helps you too.

The Best Way to Avoid, Fix, or Prevent Making This Mistake
When it comes to avoiding the critical mistake of relying solely on intuition to define your ideal client, the best solution is undeniably to prioritize gathering data to develop a detailed client avatar profile. Taking this actionable solution requires you to be intentional about getting to know your ideal client.

As a small business owner and the marketing voice behind your brand, it is vital to define your target audience to know more about them than a basic set of demographics. You need to collect data on their behaviors, preferences, and pain points. The only way to determine what those are is through well-thought-out market research.

To fix this mistake, begin by crafting a detailed customer profile that reflects your current nuanced understanding of your ideal client. Use this as a foundation to update your business and marketing plans.

Next choose one of these tactics to grow your knowledge:

1. Network with industry experts – Networking provides unparalleled insights into the latest market trends and evolving customer preferences.

2. Conduct surveys or focus groups to gather feedback on your offers to determine if they resonate with your audience.

3. Engage in strategic partnerships or collaborations to broaden your reach and introduce your business to previously untapped customer groups.

4. Leverage data analytics tools to analyze customer behavior to get a clear, data-driven picture of your clients' preferences.

Incorporating these strategies can support your business' growth and development. Real-brand examples underscore the power of this approach.

1. **Warby Parker**, a direct-to-consumer eyeglasses brand that effectively leveraged customer feedback to expand its product range and elevate the customer experience.

2. **Stitch Fix**, an online personal styling service, continuously adapts its offers based on detailed customer data to better meet their audience's preferences.

3. **Airbnb** has utilized competitor analysis to uncover market gaps and fine-tune their strategies to engage more effectively with their target customers.

Don't be fooled into thinking these are big business marketing tactics that won't work for your small business. These success stories underscore how businesses can transform a potential misstep into an opportunity for growth by employing smart, data-driven business development strategies.

Committing to investing time and resources into understanding your target audience will undeniably yield long-term rewards. By relying on data rather than intuition, you can avoid, fix, or ultimately prevent the mistake of defining your client profile based on unfounded assumptions.

Helpful Resources

There is an abundance of tools available to help entrepreneurs and small business owners efficiently conduct market research and understand their target audience.

- 101 Questions to Define your Ideal Customer Avatar workbook is a tool you can use to increase clarity and gain a deeper understanding of who your ideal client is.
  - ➢ See Chapter 8 Resources for look to this tool.

- **SurveyMonkey** is an easy-to-use tool that can help you fill in the blanks in your workbook. Gathering quantitative take is an excellent way to understand their purchasing behaviors, demographics, and preferences.

- **The Ideal Client Map online companion members area** – Chapter 8
  - ➢ Access Resources here: https://resources.theidealclientmap.com

- **TICM Online Training:** The Ideal Client Map Online Training is a visual tool and training that helps you 'see' the emotional relationships of your Ideal Client Avatar.

- Without a visual tool it takes a ton of brain power to keep all the data, and the emotional relationships, on 'top of mind'.
- Stop using words to keep track of emotions and the emotional triggers.
- Start using visuals to make it easy.

Take the time to explore these tools or similar ones to gain a deeper understanding of your target audience so you can make informed business decisions based on data rather than intuition.

Anza's #1 Piece of Advice

Here's my biggest piece of advice on this issue: Don't rely on sheer intuition alone! Incorporate market research into your marketing routine to accurately define and regularly update your ideal client profile.

It's crucial to conduct market research to accurately understand your target audience as they are today AND who they become as they use your products and services. Relying solely on intuition rather than data to define your ideal client can lead to costly mistakes and missed opportunities.

Market research does more than just define your ideal customer avatar it also helps you identify market trends, competition, and potential demand for your products or services. Data allows you to understand your audience on a deeper level, including their buying behaviors, pain points, and preferences.

Without correct data, you may misjudge your audience's needs and desires, leading to ineffective marketing strategies and products that do not resonate with your target market.

Taking the time to conduct thorough market research may seem daunting or unnecessary, however, the benefits far outweigh the effort. It can save you time and money and ensure that your business is well-aligned with the needs of your target audience. The power of informed decisions cannot be overstated—make market research your foundation and build your business on solid ground.

What We Covered

- Avoid relying solely on intuition for defining target audience
- Prioritize collection and analysis of data to develop an accurate client profile
- Data-driven approach leads to more focused and effective marketing
- Investment in understanding your target audience through data pays off in the long run
- Always rely on data, not just intuition, for client profile development and updating

What Did You Learn?

1. Understanding your ideal client's demographics is more important than understanding buying motivations and specific pain points. True / False

2. As a small business owner, it is vital to define your target audience by collecting data on their behaviors, preferences, and ___________.

3. What is the proactive approach that Anza encourages you to take?
   A. Wait for your competitors to make a move
   B. Refine your client profile
   C. Develop a weak branding and marketing strategy
   D. Ignore any new information

4. Leveraging data analytics tools can help you analyze customer behavior and get a clear, _______________-driven picture of your clients' preferences.

5. Anza's key takeaway from her failed FB ad campaign is to prioritize understanding the ideal client better than they understand themselves. True / False

6. What can cloud our judgment and lead us to make incorrect assumptions about our target audience?
   A. Biases, assumptions, and limited experiences
   B. Thorough market research and data analysis

C. Precision in deciphering target audience preferences
D. All of the above

7. Warby Parker effectively leveraged customer feedback to expand its product range and elevate the customer ______________.

Find the Answer Key in the Online Companion Members Area

As we've seen, relying solely on intuition can lead to misconceptions about your target audience's needs and buying habits. However, this is not the only factor impacting a business's success. In the next chapter, we will explore the dangers of ignoring your competition's ideal client and positioning strategies, and why understanding this is crucial for staying ahead in the market. Keep reading to discover the critical impact of this overlooked mistake on business success.

"Competitive Blindness"

Neglecting to Study Your Rivals' Target Audience

Overlooking your rivals' target audience and branding strategies can lead to "competitive blindness."

It's easy to get caught up in the excitement of developing your own client profile and branding strategy. However, one of the biggest mistakes I see small business owners make is overlooking their competitors' target audience and branding strategies. This can lead to what is known as "competitive blindness," a phenomenon where businesses fail to acknowledge the impact of their competitors and the needs and wants of their target audience.

When small business owners aren't aware of their rivals' target audience and branding strategies, they miss out on crucial insights into their own ideal clients' needs, desires, and pain points. By failing to analyze their competitor's market positioning and messaging, they risk losing their competitive edge.

In my consulting business, I have seen entrepreneurs and small business owners make this mistake for many reasons:

1. Developing their own brand identity is so consuming that they choose not to research and understand their competitors' strategies. Which is often due to a lack of awareness about the competitive landscape or an inability to differentiate themselves.

2. Their intuition tells them they know their target audience well enough, leading them to believe that it's not necessary to study their competitors' target audience. This misconception can blind them to valuable insights that can improve their own marketing and branding tactics.

3. Many business owners simply don't have the time or resources to conduct a thorough competitor analysis. With the day-to-day demands of starting up and running a business, it's common to overlook the importance of this step.

Entrepreneurs and small business owners typically make this mistake when they are in the infant stages of business development or when experiencing periods of rapid growth. In the early stages, there is often a sense of urgency to go to market as quickly as possible, which narrows their focus to internal branding efforts at the expense of competitor analysis. During growth spurts, businesses often become preoccupied with scaling their operations and meeting increasing demands, leaving little time for competitor research.

Consequences:
By not understanding who your competitors are targeting and how they are positioning themselves in the market, you are essentially flying blind and making decisions that are not grounded in data or reality. Think of it as navigating

a winding mountain road without a road map while wearing a blindfold—not only is it ill-advised, but it's also exceedingly risky.

Without this vital knowledge, you are oblivious to strategic insights that could guide your business' positioning and client targeting. Without these insights, you may find yourself investing in strategies that miss the mark, wasting valuable resources, and falling behind competitors who have a clear vision of their target market.

The consequences of overlooking your competitors' target audience and branding strategies could have more impact than you think. In today's digital business landscape, understanding your competitors and their customers is crucial for success. Not doing so can result in being left behind and struggling to grow your business.

Most importantly, not being aware of your competitor's branding strategy can lead to a lack of differentiation and a failure to stand out in the minds of potential customers. In today's marketplace consumers are inundated with endless possibilities, and being just another choice is not enough.

Let Me (Anza) Tell You a Story About a Time I Failed to Research and Fully Understand My Competitor's Target Audience

In the early stages of my coaching career, my enthusiasm was evident. I was brimming with excitement to put out my first offer, confident that it would be a game-changer. Having supported several esteemed coaches through my Virtual Business Services company, I felt an overwhelming sense of preparedness.

My ideal client mirrored those of the coaches I had previously assisted, and I was convinced of my understanding of their needs and desires. This enthusiasm, coupled with a bit of overconfidence, led me to believe I could bypass doing my own market research. I rationalized that this would save time and propel me faster toward success.

At that point, I was running retreats designed to elevate intimacy between couples by enhancing their communication skills. Just imagine the serene, white-sand beaches of Barbados, private villas with a designated butler to tend to all of your needs, and a private soaking pool to relax. A perfect romantic getaway to focus on building a stronger relationship with your significant other.

I was certain that the all-inclusive resort I had selected was the perfect backdrop for my value-packed agenda. I envisioned couples reconnecting under the golden sunsets, discovering new depths in their relationships. Everything seemed perfect on paper, and I thought the luxurious ambiance would only enhance their experience.

Where was the disconnect?
Potential clients began comparing my retreat with similar programs offered by competitors. My price point was significantly higher, despite including similar transformational experiences.

In my excitement, I had completely overlooked an essential aspect of market research—understanding the level of accommodations my target audience preferred. It wasn't that the couples weren't interested in what I was offering; rather, they placed a different value on their accommodation preferences. Had I taken the time to thoroughly research and analyze my competitors and audience, I would have discovered a trend toward more cost-effective venues, which might have included fewer frills but provided the core benefits couples sought.

This oversight was a stark and humbling revelation. It became abundantly clear that my preferences could not be generalized to my ideal client base. Just because I enjoyed the lavish experience of a 4-5 star hotel it did not mean my ideal clients did too. This was an invaluable and costly lesson—never assume you know your audience without doing the groundwork. Thorough research is not a step to be skipped; it's an indispensable part of crafting an offer that truly resonates...and sells!

The Best Way to Avoid, Fix, or Prevent Making This Mistake
Let's start by acknowledging a crucial component of business success: the power of strategic market research

and analysis. Ignoring your competition's ideal client and positioning strategies can lead to missed opportunities and stagnation. The key lies in being aware of your competitors' tactics, understanding *their* audiences, and learning from their successes and failures.

The first step in rectifying this oversight is to conduct thorough market research focused on your direct competitors. Let's take a look at four steps you can take to get started:

1. Examine every facet of their operations, from their websites to their value propositions, and identify the audiences they are engaging with. Scrutinize their messaging strategies. By familiarizing yourself with their content—blogs, articles, case studies, and white papers—you can pinpoint areas they've missed and capitalize on those gaps with your fresh perspectives and superior solutions. This comprehensive understanding will allow you to position your offers more effectively.

2. Analyze your competitors' positioning strategies. How do they market themselves? What is their core message? Check out their social media profiles to observe their content strategy and audience engagement levels. Mimicking successful tactics from competitors, while avoiding their shortcomings, can significantly strengthen your relationship with

your audience. This insight will guide you in nurturing a more loyal and engaged customer base.

3. Read competitor reviews and testimonials. These platforms offer a goldmine of information about the customer experience. Trends in praises and complaints can illustrate what your target market values and where there are persistent gaps. Addressing these pain points proactively in your offers can attract loyal customers who feel heard and valued. Strive to turn these insights into actionable plans that elevate customer satisfaction levels.

4. Monitor and adapt your content strategies based on your competitors' ad campaigns. Analyzing their digital ads can reveal emotional triggers, visuals, and calls-to-action (CTAs) that resonate with your shared audiences. Note the platforms and placements they use, as these decisions are instrumental to their overall marketing success. By gaining these insights, you can craft a far more strategic and impactful marketing approach that captivates your potential clients.

By actively leveraging your competition's ideal client base and positioning strategies, you can innovate and make your offers stand out. **I'm not advocating copying what your competitors are doing**, but rather drawing inspiration and adapting what works well for your specific branding voice. This proactive approach to market research not only avoids the costly mistake of neglecting or overlooking competitive insights; it transforms it into an opportunity for significant growth and differentiation.

Helpful Resources

- Use brand and social media monitoring tools: Tools like Mention allow you to monitor mentions and social media engagement. This information can help you understand how your competitors are perceived by their audience and the strategies they are using to engage with them.

- Stay updated on industry trends and news through tools like Google Alerts to ensure you are aware of any shifts in the market or new competition entering the field.

- **The Ideal Client Map online companion members area** – Chapter 9
    - Access Resources here: https://resources.theidealclientmap.com

- **Ideal Client Map Workbook** – available soon in the member's area

Take the time to explore these tools or similar alternatives. Understanding your competitors' target audience and branding strategies will help you develop an accurate client profile and avoid making costly mistakes in the future.

Anza's #1 Piece of Advice

Here's my take on this mistake: Don't be an ostrich with your head in the sand!

Be proactive and intentional about studying and analyzing your competitors' target audience and branding strategies to gain a better understanding of who your potential customers are. By doing so, you can identify gaps in the market, more opportunities, and threats that could affect your business. This data will help you tailor your branding and marketing strategies to better appeal to your target audience and differentiate yourself from your competitors. I encourage you to take action on what you've learned in this chapter by conducting your own research. Use this information to refine your client avatar profile and develop a strong branding and marketing strategy that will set your business apart. This proactive approach will help you stay ahead of the competition and attract the 'right' customers to your business

What We Covered

- Understand competitors' target audience and branding strategies
- Conduct thorough market research and analysis
- Avoid overlooking competitors' strategies

- Ensure comprehensive and well-informed client profile
- Lead to more effective marketing and business decisions

What Did You Learn?

1. What is "competitive blindness"?
   A. Failing to understand who your customers are
   B. Failing to understand who your competitors are targeting and how they are positioning themselves in the market
   C. Failing to understand your own branding strategy
   D. Failing to understand the impact of your competitors

2. Thorough research is an indispensable part of crafting an offer that truly resonates and _____.

3. Anza's lack of research led her to overlook the type of accommodations her target audience preferred. True / False

4. What does the author compare failing to understand competitors' target audience and branding strategies to?
   A. Navigating a winding mountain road without a map while blindfolded
   B. Navigating a straight road with a map

   C. Navigating a mountain road with a map

D. Navigating a mountain road without a map

5. By familiarizing yourself with your competitor's content—blogs, articles, case studies, and white papers—you can pinpoint areas they've missed and capitalize on those ______________ with your fresh perspectives and superior solutions.

6. Anza's mistake taught her the importance of doing thorough market research. True / False

7. What insight can studying competitors' target audience and branding strategies provide?
   A. Understanding of your own ideal clients' needs, desires, and pain points
   B. Potential differentiation and a unique value proposition
   C. Valuable strategic insights that could guide your business' positioning
   D. All of the above

Find the Answer Key in the Online Companion Members Area

As we have seen, overlooking competitors' target audience and branding strategies can be detrimental to your business. Now, let's take a look at the crucial mistake of not considering the ideal client's buying journey and decision-making process, a key aspect in ensuring the success of your business. By mapping out this journey, you can identify opportunities to address pain points, answer critical questions, and build trust with your potential clients. Stick with us as we explore practical methods to guide your ideal clients seamlessly through their buyer's journey, ensuring not just one-time transactions, but lasting relationships and loyalty.

"Driving While Blindfolded"

Failing to See Through Your Client's Eyes

Ignoring Your Ideal Client's Buying Journey and Decision-Making Can Impact Your Bottom Line

We spend a lot of time, energy, and resources creating products or services to serve our target audience. This enthusiasm has the potential to blind us to the most crucial part of achieving business success: understanding who our ideal clients really are. Ignoring our ideal client's buying journey and decision-making process is like driving a car while blindfolded—we're navigating without knowing the route or destination, a surefire recipe for disaster. Recognizing the critical importance of our ideal client's journey is not just good business sense; it is the compass that guides us toward building customer loyalty.

Understanding our ideal client's buying journey and decision-making process is not merely a box to check off; it is essential for creating content that converts. When we place ourselves in our client's shoes, we gain valuable insights into their needs, pain points, motivations, and triggers. This deep understanding allows us to tailor our marketing strategies, product offers, and customer service in ways that build trust.

Why do entrepreneurs and small business owners overlook their ideal client's buyer's journey?

In my consulting business I have come across many reasons why small business owners skip this step:

1. Many are so consumed by their vision and mission that they overlook stepping back and reviewing their offers through their client's eyes.

2. They allow their assumptions and ideas about their ideal client avatar to lead their decision-making without dedicating time to research and analysis.

3. Some lack the relevant knowledge or experience to even know what the buyer's journey is, let alone how to structure it.

4. Figuring out this information without a point of reference is overwhelming.

5. The demands of running a business put strategic planning and client research on the back burner.

Entrepreneurs and small business owners tend to make this mistake in two stages of growing their business:

1. During the early stages of their business when defining their target market and while their ideal client profile is still a work in progress.

2. When experiencing a decline in sales the scramble to reverse the trend can overshadow the need to understand the underlying issue.

Your ideal client's buyer's journey may be similar to yours, however, it is crucial to slow down and look at your process through their eyes to dispel any wrong assumptions you may have.

Consequences:
It's not just a matter of missing out on a few sales here and there. Ignoring your ideal client's buying journey can lead to a significant loss of revenue and you may risk damaging your brand's reputation making it difficult to attract new business in the future. Without a deep understanding of your ideal client's needs and desires, you won't be able to effectively market and sell your products or services. This can result in wasted time, resources, and effort as you struggle to reach an audience that simply isn't enticed by the buying triggers you created. Building a reputable brand takes time but losing it can happen in an instant—don't let ignoring your ideal client's buying journey become your stumbling block.

Let Me (Anza) Share a Story about Learning about the Concept of the Buyer's Journey
When I was growing up, my family owned an appliance and electronics store that was the go-to place for major home appliances, TVs, and stereo systems. It was much more than a business; it was the heartbeat of our small

community. Back then, we didn't toss around buzzwords like 'client avatar' or 'buyer's journey.' However, these concepts were inherently ingrained in the way we approached our customers. The aim was not just to sell but to build relationships and solve real-life problems.

Fast forward to when I was 11 years old, a revolutionary product arrived: the microwave oven. My Dad, ever the visionary, knew that this innovation would appeal primarily to women. However, the concept of cooking food rapidly in a microwave seemed almost magical, if not outright unbelievable. Convincing our target audience required more than just a sales pitch; it demanded engagement and education. My Dad had the uncanny ability to understand our customers' hesitations and needs even before they walked into the store.

Recognizing the skepticism around microwave ovens, my dad devised a brilliant strategy. We needed to show—not just tell—how this appliance would revolutionize daily cooking. The promise was clear: save time, reduce kitchen heat during sweltering summer months, and keep the same delicious quality of home-cooked meals. These were compelling benefits, yet they had to be proven to be believed. The microwave wasn't just an appliance; it was a ticket to a more efficient and comfortable life.

We said 'hello' to the Saturday morning cooking demonstration class, our innovative solution to win trust and spark curiosity. Every week, we hosted classes where we showed potential customers how to prepare everything from a simple cup of tea to an elaborate full meal using only a microwave. Women from all over town flocked to these sessions, intrigued and excited by the prospect of modern convenience. These classes became a staple in our business as we built a sense of camaraderie among the attendees and created an atmosphere of shared learning and discovery.

The success of these cooking classes was nothing short of phenomenal. Sales saw a significant boost, but more importantly, we built an invaluable trust with our community. Our store became synonymous not just with quality appliances, but with genuine care and customer support. We tapped into a network of referrals that might have eluded us had we not taken the time to understand and solve our customers' problems. This experience taught me the irreplaceable value of connecting deeply and communicating effectively with our ideal client.

Reflecting back, those Saturday classes did more than just introduce a new appliance to potential customers. They were a masterclass in relationship-building and effective communication, lessons that continue to inspire me to this day. They taught me that when you truly understand your audience, meet their needs with genuine solutions, and communicate your message authentically, you not only achieve business success but also create lasting bonds. It's a timeless strategy that is still as relevant to me now as it was back then.

The Best Way to Avoid, Fix, or Prevent Making This Mistake

Let's face it—we've all made mistakes in our journey to attract and retain the right clients. The good news is that recognizing these missteps offers an opportunity to pause and regroup. If you've realized that you haven't been considering your ideal client's buying journey and decision-making process, it's not the end of the world. The key to fixing this oversight lies in gathering more specific data about your ideal client avatar before you build your funnels.

Here are three steps to get you started:

1. **Conduct market research to understand their buying triggers.**
   Get your hands dirty with surveys, one-on-one interviews, and analyzing customer feedback. Use standardized questions so you're comparing apples to apples. It's within these granular details that you'll uncover invaluable insights. Knowing exactly what motivates your clients and how they make decisions allows you to craft strategies that speak to their specific buying language. This foundational understanding transforms guesswork into educated targeting, paving the way for more meaningful engagements and higher conversions.

2. **Use Focus Groups.**
   Recruit participants who reflect your target demographic. Hire a skilled moderator to steer the

conversation so you can ensure that every voice is heard, and every detail is captured. This structured approach not only reveals subtle buying triggers it also builds a connection with your audience, showing them that their opinions matter. Dive into their experiences, listen to their stories, and watch as the nuances of their decision-making process come to light which will guide you to create more focused marketing campaigns.

3. **Leverage CRM software.**
   Software like GoHighLevel is crucial for tracking and analyzing the behavior and interactions of your leads and customers. This technology offers a 360-degree view of your client's journey, allowing you to understand the touchpoints that matter most. Engage more effectively through timely follow-ups, personalized emails, and targeted offers that cater to their evolving needs. The data gleaned from a CRM can offer eye-opening insights, helping you make informed decisions on how to engage with your leads more effectively and efficiently.

By taking these steps, you can overcome this mistake. Once you have this gold mine of data, you'll be able to build a pipeline filled with highly qualified leads and satisfied customers who feel seen and understood. It's never too late to course-correct and shift your strategy to better serve your clients and grow your business.

Helpful Resources

It's crucial to understand and cater to your ideal client's buying journey and decision-making process to convert leads into paying customers. Thankfully, there are tons of specialized tools designed to streamline this process.

- **The Ideal Client Map online companion members area** – Chapter 10
    - Access Resources here: https://resources.theidealclientmap.com

- **Website and Behavioral Analytics Tools**
  Analytics and reporting tools like Google Analytics track website visitor behavior, helping you understand how users navigate your site, which pages they visit, and what actions they take.

- **Email Marketing and Automation Tools.**
  Programs like AWeber provide advanced email marketing, automation, and CRM features to understand and engage with your audience. They also have A/B testing tools to allow you to experiment with different approaches to determine the most effective strategy.

Exploring and utilizing these tools can ensure you are meeting your client's needs and preferences effectively, ultimately leading to stronger, more personalized connections and increased conversion rates.

Anza's #1 Piece of Advice

Don't put the cart before the horse and start creating new products or services you *think* will resonate with your target audience. While a strong offering is important, it's meaningless if it doesn't align with the ideal client's needs and buying triggers. When it comes to generating more highly qualified leads, you can't overlook your ideal client's buying journey and decision-making process. The key to creating a successful lead generation strategy is understanding the path your potential customers take from awareness to purchase. It's more than just the steps they go through, it's also about their emotional and cognitive engagement at each stage. Recognizing these nuances enables you to craft messages and offers that resonate deeply, addressing their specific needs and concerns at just the right moments.

This means creating content and messaging that speaks directly to their pain points, wants, needs, and desires at each stage of their journey. For instance, if a customer is just starting to explore options, educational content can position you as a knowledgeable resource. As they move closer to making a decision, case studies, testimonials, and personalized consultations can entice them to choose your product or service. Don't forget to segment your lists so you can send the right message at the right time to guide them through their purchasing decision process.

What We Covered

- Don't ignore your ideal client's buying journey
- Take the time to understand your ideal client's buyer's decision-making triggers
- Tailor marketing and sales efforts to better align with client needs
- Gather customer feedback and conduct market research
- Put yourself in your ideal client's shoes to ensure strategies are effective and serve their needs

What Did You Learn?

1. If a customer is just starting to explore options, educational content can position you as a _________ resource.

2. When do entrepreneurs and small business owners tend to make the mistake of overlooking their ideal client's buyer's journey?
   A. During the early stages of their business
   B. While experiencing a decline in sales
   C. Both A and B
   D. None of the above

3. The concept of the buyer's journey was not important in the way Anza's family approached their customers. True / False

4. When it comes to generating more highly qualified leads, you can't overlook your ideal client's buying journey and _______________ process.

5. Why is it essential to understand your ideal client's buying journey for creating content that converts?
   A. It allows tailoring marketing strategies and product offers
   B. It provides valuable insights into your client's needs, pain points, motivations, and triggers
   C. It helps in building trust with potential clients
   D. All of the above

6. What approach did Anza's family take to convince customers about the benefits of the microwave oven?
   A. Sales pitch
   B. Engagement and education
   C. Aggressive advertising
   D. Demonstrating other products.

7. The key to creating a successful lead generation strategy is understanding the path your potential customers take from _____________ to purchase.

Find the Answer Key in the Online Companion Members Area

As we have seen, not considering your ideal client's buying journey can lead to missed opportunities and lost sales. In the following chapter, we will explore the mistake of misreading clients' preferred touchpoints, shedding light on the crucial role of aligning with clients' preferred channels of communication and interaction. Keep reading to discover how this oversight can impact your business success.

"The Hidden Highway"

Misreading Clients' Preferred Touchpoints

You don't have to guess where your ideal clients hang out online.

One of the most critical aspects of running a successful business is knowing where your ideal clients spend their time online. Without this knowledge, marketing your products or services effectively can feel like driving a winding mountain road in the dark with no headlights. Many business owners fall into the trap of guesswork when it comes to figuring out where their target audience hangs out leading to disappointing marketing results.

Guessing where to connect with your ideal clients on the internet is an all-too common and costly error. This approach waters down your messaging and reduces the chance of catching the attention of your ideal client. Such a broad approach is not only inefficient, but also highly ineffective. Guessing translates into wasted time, energy, and missed opportunities to engage with potential clients who are genuinely interested in what you have to offer.

Why do small business owners make this mistake?

One primary reason this guessing game continues to frustrate small business owners is the lack of understanding of their target audience. While they may have a broad idea of their ideal clients based on a gut feeling, they often do not truly understand the specific needs, preferences, and behaviors of this group of people. This lack of data-driven insight leads to even the best marketing strategies not producing results due to a disconnect with the audience's actual online behavior.

Another factor that leads to this mistake is the pressure of starting and running a business. New business owners often take the path of least resistance which bypasses research and relies purely on their gut instinct. The excitement and urgency of starting a business can overshadow the need for strategic planning and in-depth research, resulting in poor decisions.

Consequences:
When you guess where your ideal clients actually spend their time online, you are missing out on the chance to build meaningful connections and relationships with them. Imagine trying to strike up a conversation at a party, but you showed up at the wrong location altogether! Your genuine attempts to engage and connect with your target audience will fall flat, leading to missed opportunities for building trust and loyalty. In the digital space, trust is the cornerstone of customer relationships, and without it, converting leads into loyal customers becomes an uphill battle.

The online spaces your ideal clients frequent are treasure troves of information, revealing their needs, preferences, and pain points. When you're in the wrong digital neighborhood, you miss these vital cues, blinding you to what truly drives your audience's decisions. It’s like trying to navigate in a new city without a map – you might eventually reach your destination, but the journey will take considerably longer.

Let Me (Anza) share a Client Story of How Casting a Net Too Wide Tanked Her Results

Meet Beth, an accomplished law enforcement officer with a remarkable track record, looking to start her second career as an executive coach after her retirement. Beth envisioned leveraging her extensive experience and unique insights to help individuals navigate their professional paths successfully. It was during this transition phase that our paths crossed, as she was gearing up to launch her first summit—an ambitious endeavor that aimed to bring together a community eager for her guidance and expertise.

When we first connected, Beth was employing a framework I was quite familiar with. This provided a perfect opportunity for me to dive in and help her orchestrate the complexities of her online event. Our shared understanding of the framework allowed us to synchronize effortlessly, ensuring that we navigated each component with precision and clarity. My experience with this particular model had previously yielded stellar results, making me confident that Beth was on the right track.

However, a significant challenge lay ahead. Unlike my previous clients who had large mailing lists and a solid client base, Beth was starting from scratch. She didn't have a database of former clients or business besties who would promote her event. This lack of a foundational network posed a notable hurdle, as summits often rely heavily on an existing audience or collaborative promotions to gain traction and drive attendance.

Beth decided to rely mainly on Facebook ads and the email lists of her event's speakers, hoping they would promote the summit to their followers. While this approach had the potential to expand her reach, it was substantially riskier. The absence of her audience meant she had limited control overreach and engagement, placing all bets on external promotions and the performance of her ads.

The execution of the summit went off without a hitch. Beth adhered closely to the prescribed system, resulting in a seamless operation. Yet, despite a polished and professional event, the response was not as she had hoped. There were no conversions. This outcome stemmed largely from an unclear understanding of her ideal client and their online hangouts and habits. Without this crucial insight, she struggled to craft targeted messaging to attract the right audience.

The failure of her Facebook ads to connect with the desired demographic was a costly lesson, underscoring the importance of knowing one's audience inside and out. This experience proved to be a catalyst for Beth, prompting her to pause and reassess her strategy. It highlighted the need to define her ideal avatar meticulously and understand where to find them. Beth's journey, while initially fraught with challenges, set her on a path of focused refinement, ensuring her future endeavors would be more aligned, targeted, and successful.

The Best Way to Avoid, Fix, or Prevent Making This Mistake
The only solution to avoid aimlessly guessing where your ideal clients might be online is to conduct market research to identify the exact places they hang out. This approach is crucial because it increases your chances of directly connecting with and building relationships with your target audience. Once you know where they are you can tailor your marketing efforts to focus on the exact platforms, they spend time on.

To start implementing this solution take a look at your ideal client's age, ethnicity, income, education, community, and political affiliations. These factors all play a role in where they choose to spend their time online. With this comprehensive understanding, you can pinpoint various online platforms and communities where they are most active. This could range from popular social media networks to specialized industry forums, niche websites, or specific online groups.

Here's some basic info from the Pew Research Center info to get you started:

	18 – 29	30 – 49	50 – 64	65+
Age	Facebook: 67% Instagram: 78% LinkedIn: 32% YouTube: 93% TikTok: 62%	Facebook: 75% Instagram: 59% LinkedIn: 40% YouTube: 92% TikTok: 39%	Facebook: 69% Instagram: 35% LinkedIn: 40% YouTube: 83% TikTok: 24%	Facebook: 58% Instagram: 15% LinkedIn: 12% YouTube: 60% TikTok: 10%
Gender (not age specific)	Facebook: Instagram: LinkedIn: YouTube: TikTok:	men 59% men 39% men 31% men 82% men 25%	women 76% women 54% women 29% women 83% women 40%	
Ethnicity (not age specific)	White Facebook: 69% Instagram: 43% LinkedIn: 30% YouTube: 81% TikTok: 28%	Black Facebook: 64% Instagram: 46% LinkedIn: 46% YouTube: 82% TikTok: 39%	Hispanic Facebook: 66% Instagram: 58% LinkedIn: 58% YouTube: 86% TikTok: 49%	Asian Facebook: 67% Instagram: 57% LinkedIn: 57% YouTube: 93% TikTok: 29%
Income (not age specific)	Facebook: Instagram: LinkedIn: YouTube: TikTok:	$30-69K 70% $30-69K 46% $30-69K 19% $30-69K 83% $30-69K 37%	$70-99K 74% $70-99K 49% $70-99K 34% $70-99K 86% $70-99K 34%	$100+K 68% $100+K 54% $100+K 53% $100+K 89% $100+K 27%
Education (not age specific)	Facebook: Instagram: LinkedIn: YouTube: TikTok:	High Sch 63% High Sch 37% High Sch 10% High Sch 74% High Sch 35%	College 71% College 50% College 28% College 85% College 38%	Grad 70% Grad 55% Grad 53% Grad 89% Grad 26%
Community (not age specific)	Facebook: Instagram: LinkedIn: YouTube: TikTok:	Urban 66% Urban 53% Urban 31% Urban 85% Urban 36%	Suburban 68% Suburban 49% Suburban 35% Suburban 85% Suburban 31%	Rural 70% Rural 38% Rural 18% Rural 77% Rural 33%
Political Affiliation (not age specific)	Facebook: Instagram: LinkedIn: YouTube: TikTok:	Rep 70% Rep 43% Rep 29% Rep 82% Rep 30%	Dem 67% Dem 53% Dem 34% Dem 84% Dem 36%	

Note: Not all platforms are listed in this chart. Visit the Member's Area for success to the full report.

Use the following examples to see how this strategy could work to connect with people in your target audience:

1. **A fitness coach targeting busy professionals.** LinkedIn becomes your goldmine; it's a platform flooded with career-driven individuals who are constantly seeking ways to balance a hectic work life with supporting their health goals. By being present and active there, you can offer value that resonates with their specific needs.

2. **A small business offering eco-friendly products.** Your ideal clients are likely passionate about environmental conservation. Join groups on Facebook dedicated to sustainable living and green initiatives. Engaging in these communities allows you to take part in focused conversations, helping you build credibility and trust with an audience that cares deeply about what you're offering.

3. **A freelance graphic designer** yearning to collaborate with startups, platforms like Upwork or Fiverr are the perfect arenas. Here, entrepreneurs actively seek creative professionals to bring their branding and design visions to life. Your presence on these platforms makes it easy for them to find you, ensuring a steady stream of potential clients who appreciate and need your skills.

4. **A life coach specializing in personal development**, online platforms like Reddit or Quora offer rich

opportunities. People flock to these spaces looking for advice, support, and inspiration to improve their mindset and achieve personal goals. By engaging thoughtfully on these platforms, you can showcase your expertise, offer actionable advice, and connect with individuals genuinely interested in personal growth.

By identifying and engaging on the specific platforms where your ideal clients hang out online, you not only place your business in front of the right people, you also build a foundation for creating lasting relationships. This nuanced understanding and strategic positioning will ultimately convert leads into loyal customers.

Helpful Resources

I'll be the first to admit that research is tedious and time consuming, but it's necessary if you want to get better results from your marketing efforts. If you're not sure where your ideal clients are hanging out online, it's time to pause and gather some data to get the answers you need to connect with the right people.

Here are three tools you can use to get answers quickly:

- **The Ideal Client Map online companion members area** – Chapter 11
  - ➢ Access Resources here: https://resources.theidealclientmap.com

- **Social media analytics**: Use analytics tools provided by platforms such as Facebook, Instagram, and LinkedIn to see where your engagement and followers are coming from. This will help you understand which platforms are most valuable for finding your ideal clients.

- **Website analytics**: By using tools like Google Analytics, you can gain valuable insights into how visitors are finding and interacting with your website. This data can help you better understand where your ideal clients are coming from and where they are most likely to engage with your brand.

- **101 Questions to Define Your Ideal Customer Avatar workbook**: By asking curious questions about your ideal avatar, you will create a clear picture of who they are as a real-life person. When you have one person in mind, it is easier to find out where they hang out online.

- **Ideal Client Map - Chapter 11**:
  - ➢ Plug this info into the blue avatar data box

Anza's #1 Piece of Advice

To pinpoint your ideal client's online hangouts, mere guesswork won't cut it. My best advice on this topic is to get your hands dirty with some serious research and dive deep into my "101 Questions to Define Your Ideal Customer Avatar" workbook. This isn't just busywork—it's a crucial step in steering your marketing efforts in the right direction. The magic formula to successful marketing and client acquisition hinges on knowing exactly where your target audience spends their time online. Without such targeted knowledge, your outreach could very well miss its mark, costing you both time and resources.

Relying on assumptions is a risky business strategy that can lead to wasted efforts and missed opportunities. Think about it: would you rather gamble with your marketing budget on vague guesses, or make informed decisions backed by solid data?

I hope you said, "Informed decisions based on solid data." To gather this indispensable data, you'll need to invest time to:

- Conduct surveys,
- Analyze website traffic patterns, and
- Study social media engagement metrics.

This type of research allows you to pinpoint where your potential clients are most active online. These insights will help you align your marketing efforts to strike precisely where your audience lives, magnifying the impact of your campaigns.

Understanding your ideal clients' online hangouts isn't just beneficial—it's essential. Without this knowledge, you risk squandering opportunities to interact with potential customers and, more importantly, to build lasting relationships. It's not just about visibility; it's about engagement AND connection.

Conduct your research with diligence and enthusiasm, and you'll be able to design marketing strategies that speak directly to your target audience's hearts and minds. This strategic alignment will attract potential clients who genuinely resonate with your brand and improve your conversion rates.

Remember, every moment spent on research is an investment in your business's future success. By implementing data-driven marketing tactics, you'll see an uptick in engagement and conversions, driving substantial results for your business and cultivating stronger client relationships. So, don't wait—take what you've learned in this chapter and take your marketing plan to the next level.

What We Covered

- Guessing or assuming where your ideal clients hang out online can waste time and resources
- To avoid this mistake, conduct thorough research and leverage data and analytics
- Engage actively with your target audience to gain insights into their online behaviors and preferences
- Make informed decisions about where to focus your marketing and outreach efforts
- Connect with your ideal clients in a more meaningful and effective way

What Did You Learn?

1. What is the ultimate goal of identifying and engaging with your target audience on specific online platforms?
   A. To have a large social media following
   B. To drive sales with aggressive marketing tactics
   C. To build lasting relationships and convert leads into loyal customers
   D. To gain popularity and recognition in online communities

2. The failure of Anza's Facebook ad campaign highlighted the importance of knowing one's target audience. True / False

3. Guessing where to connect with your ideal clients on the internet is an all-too common and costly ________

4. What is the benefit of identifying and engaging on specific online platforms where your ideal clients hang out?
   A. It gives you exposure to a wider audience
   B. It helps build trust and credibility with your target audience
   C. It helps you connect with your competitors
   D. It doesn't have any impact on your business

5. Beth struggled to create targeted messaging for her summit due to a lack of understanding of her ideal client. True / False

6. By investing time and effort to understand where your ideal clients hang out online, you set the stage for more ________________, effective, and efficient marketing efforts, ultimately driving your business toward ______________.

7. Why is trust important in the digital space?
   A. Trust is the cornerstone of customer relationships
   B. Trust is irrelevant in the digital space
   C. Trust is not needed for converting leads into loyal customers
   D. Trust is easily given

Find the Answer Key in the Online Companion Members Area

As important as it is to understand the communication channels and touchpoints preferred by your ideal clients, it's equally crucial to stay current on their changing preferences and behaviors. In the next chapter, we'll explore why it's essential to continuously update your ideal client profile to ensure you don't fall behind in reaching and satisfying your target audience. Keep reading to discover how you can stay ahead of the curve in understanding and meeting your ideal clients' evolving needs.

"Falling Behind"

Why Your Ideal Client Avatar Profile Needs an Update

Failing to update your ideal client avatar can result in major setbacks in your business.

As business owners, we know the importance of developing a strategic marketing plan that effectively targets our ideal clients. We spend endless hours crafting detailed ideal client avatar profiles, carefully examining demographics, interests, and pain points. However, many of us fail to realize that our ideal client avatar is not static; it's a dynamic, ever-evolving representation of our target market.

The mistake of forgetting to update your client avatar profile is exactly what it sounds like - neglecting to revisit and revise the characteristics of your ideal client. This mistake can be likened to navigating with an outdated road map instead of using your GPS. When you ignore the ongoing changes in your audience's characteristics, it's easy to inadvertently misalign your marketing efforts with the needs and wants of your actual clientele. Sticking rigidly to an outdated avatar means you're communicating with a segment of your audience that no longer exists, thereby diminishing the impact of your message.

Why is this oversight so detrimental to growing your business?
This mistake can have a lasting impact on your business because:

1. Market conditions and consumer behaviors are in a constant state of flux; what appealed to your audience five years ago may no longer strike a chord today. Keep in mind, your ideal client will change and grow as they use your products and services.

2. As new consumer segments emerge over time, you could miss critical opportunities to engage with these potential customers if your avatar isn't up to date.

3. A misalignment between your marketing and your actual audience can result in ineffective campaigns that fail to connect emotionally and practically with those you aim to serve.

Why do entrepreneurs and small business owners frequently make this mistake?
One reason is that many view the creation of a client avatar as a one-and-done task rather than an ongoing process. It's easy to become absorbed in the day-to-day operations of running a business, making it tempting to set this crucial activity on the back burner.

Consequences
You may think that forgetting to update your client avatar profile is a minor oversight, but the consequences could be worse than you think. Imagine casting a fishing net into a lake only to catch the wrong type of fish and having to catch and release repeatedly. This misalignment consumes energy, resources, and, most importantly, your chance for your business to thrive. In a digital market with ever-changing algorithms, what worked yesterday might not work today.

Not updating your ideal avatar profile can have several repercussions:

1. **Loss of potential customers.** As your business evolves and grows, your target audience inevitably changes. Ignoring these transformations is like selling winter coats in mid-July. Without a precise understanding of who your ideal customer is today, your marketing efforts will fall flat, missing the mark entirely.

2. **Negative effects on your brand reputation.** When your marketing campaigns are not laser-targeted, they can create confusion, leaving potential customers bewildered and dissatisfied. A misrepresented brand fails to meet expectations, leading to skepticism and eroding trust.

3. **Wasted resources and missed opportunities**. Without a clear understanding of who your ideal customer is, you may end up investing time, money, and effort into marketing strategies that don't yield the desired results which can drain your resources and hinder your ability to innovate and adapt to changing market conditions.

Let me (Anza) introduce you to Sarah...
Sarah is a charismatic and accomplished executive coach who dedicates her expertise to empowering C-Suite women. These trailblazing professionals navigate the treacherous waters of male-dominated roles, shouldering immense stress, and are driven by a relentless pursuit of success. Sarah's strategies are nothing short of transformative, helping these high-performing women rise above challenges and excel in their demanding roles.

However, despite her undeniable success and the impact she creates, Sarah feels a lingering void. Her true passion lies in supporting women burdened by the invisible weight of high stress at home, married to spouses grappling with mental illness.

Sarah's heartfelt desire to make a difference stems from her deep empathy for these women, who face burnout while managing chaotic personal lives alongside their professional pressures. They navigate their days without respite, often shrouding their struggles in silence due to the stigma surrounding mental health. Sarah knows firsthand the anguish and isolation these women endure, and she yearns to offer them a lifeline. Despite this compelling inclination, Sarah hesitates to redefine her client avatar. She recognizes that many within her current niche also silently battle these personal demons.

Yet, addressing these issues indirectly won't suffice. To truly connect with and uplift this specific segment of her target audience, Sarah must openly acknowledge the unique challenges they face at home. It is not enough to hope that her current messaging will reach them; she must recalibrate her language to address their highly specific needs. Only by doing so can she offer her invaluable guidance to help them create a peace-filled life. By bringing these stigma-filled issues to the forefront, Sarah can break the silence and instigate a meaningful dialogue that empowers women to seek and accept support.

Redefining her client profile doesn't mean abandoning her current client base. On the contrary, Sarah can continue to serve her existing clientele while strategically segmenting her communication to cater to those dealing with mental health struggles at home. This precision in messaging will not only enhance her connection with this particular group but also amplify her impact. A targeted approach ensures that her support reaches those who need it most, fostering an environment where women feel understood, supported, and emboldened to overcome their obstacles.

Ultimately, Sarah's mission is about building bridges. By updating her client profile and refining her outreach, she extends her hand more clearly and compassionately to those who might otherwise remain in the shadows.

Her work can be the beacon of hope and change for these women, creating spaces where they feel seen, heard, and healed. Sarah's journey is not just about producing stellar results but also about nurturing connections that transform lives. By aligning her professional endeavors with her soulful passion, she can thrive in her purpose, fulfilling both her and her clients' deepest needs.

The Best Way to Avoid, Fix, or Prevent Making This Mistake
The key to avoiding the oversight of not updating your ideal client avatar profile lies in having a strategic and actionable marketing plan. This approach is superior because it equips you with the knowledge to remain informed about dynamic shifts in your target market, allowing you to constantly reassess and update your client avatar profile as your business and target market evolves. Staying ahead of market trends not only keeps your business competitive but also propels you toward sustainable growth by ensuring that your offers are consistently in alignment with your client's needs.

Establishing a regular review schedule is another crucial part of your marketing plan. By committing to a quarterly or bi-annual review, you ensure that your client avatar profile is always up-to-date. This practice allows you to identify and quickly respond to changes in the market, shifts in customer preferences, or new business goals. Consistently refreshing your target strategies based on these reviews keeps your business agile and responsive, rather than reactive.

Feedback integration is another essential component. Proactively gather and incorporate feedback from your customers into your avatar profile updates. This feedback, which includes insights, complaints, and suggestions, is incredibly valuable. It provides a raw and real glimpse into the minds of your audience, offering cues for refining your understanding of who they are and what they need. When you listen to your customers and act on their feedback, you not only improve your product or service but also build trust and loyalty.

Companies like **Nike and Starbucks** have excelled at updating their ideal client avatar profiles in response to market trends. They've done this by continuously engaging with their audience through social media, collecting customer feedback, and analyzing consumer data. This proactive approach has allowed them to tailor their marketing strategies to connect with their changing target demographic. Similarly, tech giants such as Apple and Samsung regularly update their ideal client avatar profiles through rigorous market research and customer surveys. This ensures their products and marketing efforts resonate with evolving consumer preferences, enabling them to stay at the forefront of their industries.

The lesson here is clear: staying diligent and responsive to market changes is crucial for sustained success. By continuously updating your ideal client avatar profile and refining your marketing strategy, you not only avoid the pitfalls of outdated or inaccurate assumptions but also set the stage for greater engagement and growth.

Helpful Resources

- **The Ideal Client Map online companion members area** – Chapter 12
  - ➢ Access Resources here: https://resources.theidealclientmap.com

- **Survey tools** - Platforms like SurveyMonkey and Typeform enable you to gather feedback directly from your customers, helping you to validate and refine your client avatar profile. You can ask specific questions about their needs, challenges, and goals to ensure you have a clear understanding of who your target audience is.

- **The Ideal Client Map Online Training:** The Ideal Client Map Online Training is a visual tool and training that helps you 'see' the emotional relationships of your Ideal Client Avatar.
  - ➢ Without a visual tool it takes a ton of brain power to keep all the emotional data on track.

- ➢ Stop using words to keep track of emotions and the emotional triggers.
- ➢ Start using visuals to make it easy.

- **Actionable Marketing Plan Course** Look for our course in the member's area to help you create a plan that takes your marketing activities to the next level.

Anza's #1 Piece of Advice

Here's my most practical piece of advice on this issue: create a simple marketing plan that includes a schedule and tactics to update your client avatar profile as you build a marketing strategy for the future. One of the biggest mistakes small business owners make is assuming that creating a client avatar profile is a one-time activity. This complacency can lead to stagnant marketing efforts, misaligned campaigns, and missed opportunities to connect with potential customers. The foundation of a successful marketing strategy lies in an accurate and current understanding of your target audience, and this starts with an accurate client avatar profile.

It is important to remember that market trends and consumer behaviors are constantly evolving, and what may have resonated with your audience in the past may no longer be as effective. By periodically updating your client avatar profile, you can gain invaluable insights into the current needs, desires, and pain points and create a new segment within your target audience, allowing you to tailor your marketing efforts more effectively and sustainably. Think of it as an ongoing dialogue with your customers—one that enables you to stay relevant and innovative. When you pinpoint these evolving characteristics, you can refine your messaging, choose the right channels, and create resonant content that truly speaks to your client's experiences and aspirations.

Take action by setting aside time each quarter to revisit and update your client avatar profile. Use data analytics tools, customer surveys, and customer feedback to ensure that you have a clear understanding of who your audience is and what motivates them. Consider this quarterly review as an essential meeting with your most important business asset—your customers. This intentional approach will build stronger relationships and increase customer loyalty.

What We Covered

- Regularly update your client avatar profile to account for changing market needs and preferences.
- Revisit your client avatar and gather updated information about your target audience.
- Consider demographic changes, evolving consumer behaviors, and shifting industry trends when updating your client avatar.

- Conduct market research, surveys, and gather feedback from existing customers to gain valuable insights.

- Keeping your client avatar profile up to date ensures that your marketing efforts align with your target audience's needs.

What Did You Learn?

1. Why is neglecting to update your client avatar profile detrimental to growing your business?
   A. Market conditions and consumer behaviors are in a constant state of flux
   B. You could miss critical opportunities to engage with potential customers
   C. A misalignment between your marketing and your actual audience can result in ineffective campaigns
   D. All of the above

2. An outdated avatar means you're communicating with a segment of your audience that no longer ________________.

3. Sarah hesitates to redefine her client avatar because she is afraid of losing her current client base. True/False

4. What analogy is given to describe the consequences of neglecting to update your client avatar profile?
   A. Driving without a seatbelt
   B. Catching the wrong type of fish with a fishing net
   C. Taking a shot in the dark
   D. Navigating with an outdated road map

5. Neglecting to consistently update your client avatar profile can result in ineffective campaigns that fail to ________________ with those you aim to serve.

6. Redefining Sarah's client profile means abandoning her current client base. True/False

7. How can neglecting to update your client avatar profile impact your business growth?
   A. It can lead to an ineffective marketing strategy
   B. It can result in a misalignment between your marketing and your actual audience
   C. It can diminish the impact of your message
   D. All of the above

Find the Answer Key in the Online Companion Members Area

As businesses neglect to update their ideal client avatar profile, they risk losing touch with their target audience. This disconnect can lead to a breakdown in communication, ultimately causing their brand to fall out of sync with their client's language, a mistake that can have significant ramifications on their success. Keep reading to discover the impact of lost translation and how to avoid it.

"Lost in Translation"

When Your Brand Doesn't Speak Your Client's Language

It's impossible to connect with clients if your brand's core values are out of alignment with your client's beliefs.

As small business owners, we are constantly striving to connect with potential clients and expand our reach. Whether it's through marketing efforts, networking, or social media engagement, there are numerous ways in which we try to build relationships with our target audience. Yet, one crucial mistake that often slips through the cracks is the failure to align our brand values with our ideal client's beliefs. This oversight can lead to missed opportunities, failed connections, and ultimately, business stagnation.

Why is this such a big mistake?

Being out of alignment with your potential clients' beliefs creates a disconnect that's hard to bridge. When your brand doesn't resonate with your target audience's core beliefs, building trust and loyalty becomes an uphill battle. Without this alignment, the very essence of your brand fails to strike a chord, hindering your ability to achieve sustainable growth and long-term success. It's not just about selling; it's about creating relationships that foster loyalty and advocacy for your brand.

Why do entrepreneurs and small business owners make this mistake?

Entrepreneurs and small business owners struggle in this area for several reasons.

1. Lack of clarity and understanding of who your ideal client truly is. Without a well-defined understanding of your target audience, accurately aligning your brand values becomes almost impossible.

2. Prioritizing personal values over those of your ideal clients can lead to a disconnect in messaging and communication. It's easy to assume your preferences mirror those of your target audience, which can be a detrimental miscalculation.

3. Gaps in resources or knowledge needed to effectively research and understand client beliefs result in a missed opportunity to connect meaningfully with potential customers.

This mistake is especially prevalent among small business owners who are in a rush to grow their client base. The recent trend is to do it fast, get your products out there, you can fix it later. In the pursuit of expansion, the crucial step of aligning brand values with the beliefs of the ideal client is often overshadowed.

Eagerness can cause us to adopt generic marketing tactics, rather than taking the time to dig deeper into the minds and hearts of our target audience. However, investing in understanding and aligning with your ideal client's beliefs is not just a strategic move; it's a foundational step toward building a brand that not only attracts but retains its clientele.

Consequences

When you fail to connect with future clients beyond your immediate circle, you're not just missing an opportunity—you're potentially alienating a substantial segment of your potential customer base. Building relationships is the foundation of any successful business, and isolating yourself limits your reach and ultimately, your growth. Imagine the untapped potential lying just outside your current network. These are individuals who haven't yet experienced your product or service but could become some of your most loyal and valuable customers.

The consequences of this oversight are far more serious than you might initially realize. Failing to engage with a broader audience means you're missing a critical chance to align your brand values with the beliefs and needs of your ideal clients beyond your current reach. When people don't see their ideals and values reflected in your brand, you risk losing their interest, trust, and confidence. Over time, this erosion of credibility can diminish customer loyalty. A loyal customer base isn't just a steady source of revenue; it's the foundation upon which your brand's reputation is built.

Moreover, failing to connect beyond your immediate circle can hinder the growth and expansion of your business. We're living in a hyper-connected digital world where word-of-mouth and online reviews have tremendous influence. An impression of being out-of-touch can cascade into widespread perceptions that have the potential to damage your brand image. This negative perception can rapidly circulate, impeding your ability to attract new customers and grow your market share.

Let's take a deeper look at my (Anza) client Kelcey's story... Meet Kelcey, a dynamic and passionate new transformation coach with a heartfelt mission. When Kelcey and I first crossed paths, she was diligently helping women navigate significant transitions in their lives. Her empathy and heartfelt approach were unmatched, and she offered exceptional strategies tailored for the women she worked with. However, despite her robust skills and genuine desire to make an impact, she was struggling with establishing a deeper connection with her clients.

We began by engaging in an enlightening conversation about what the term 'transitions' truly encompassed. For Kelcey, it spanned a spectrum of pivotal life changes—healing from a divorce, transitioning into becoming an empty nester, or coping with a life-altering medical diagnosis. Each of these transitions carried unique emotional and psychological challenges. Despite her best efforts, Kelcey's broad approach was not resonating as deeply as she had hoped with the women who needed her guidance the most.

It became evident that the values underpinning each type of transition were distinct and thus required a more focused, personalized approach. Trying to address all these experiences with a single, all-encompassing message was resulting in a diluted impact. Women facing different types of life transitions needed to feel that Kelcey truly understood their unique situations and challenges. This realization marked a pivotal moment in Kelcey's journey as a coach.

We decided it was time for Kelcey to revisit the drawing board and pinpoint which types of transitions she felt most passionate about and equipped to specialize in. This refinement was crucial in developing a comprehensive marketing strategy. We evaluated her products and services, scrutinized the language she used, and planned how she would effectively communicate and connect with her target audience. This strategic approach ensured that Kelcey could provide the nuanced support each woman needed based on her specific life transition.

One of her major a-ha moments was recognizing that, as a woman of faith, she desired to work exclusively with Christian women. This revelation dawned on her as she realized that her deep-seated beliefs about family and end-of-life issues clashed with those of her non-Christian clients. This newfound awareness served as a pivotal turning point, dramatically realigning the trajectory of her business.

When she started to embrace her faith as the cornerstone of her professional endeavors, she began building a community where shared values built trust and understanding. The profound impact of this decision was not merely a superficial shift in clientele; it was a transformative move that brought renewed purpose, authenticity, and fulfillment to her work. As she navigated this new path, she found that aligning her business with her faith not only enhanced her professional relationships but also amplified the results she could deliver, creating a ripple effect of positive change.

The Best Way to Avoid, Fix, or Prevent Making This Mistake
Identifying the communities, organizations, or online groups that your ideal clients are part of is the first and most crucial step in establishing a meaningful connection with them. This can include online forums, social media groups, professional associations, and local community organizations. By pinpointing where your potential clients congregate, you position yourself in the midst of their conversations, preferences, and challenges. This proximity allows you to provide relevant insights, ask thought-provoking questions, and demonstrate your expertise in a way that naturally draws attention. Engagement in these communities not only amplifies your visibility but also lays the groundwork for trust and credibility.

Once you're actively engaging with these groups, it's essential to focus on understanding the core values and beliefs of the members. It's not enough to simply participate; you need to listen attentively and analyze the common themes that emerge from their discussions. This means being present, not just active, by paying attention to the language they use, the subjects that spur the most conversation, and the challenges or victories they frequently share.

The next step is to tailor your brand messaging to resonate with these newfound insights. Your communications should reflect a clear alignment with the community's ethos, demonstrating that your products or services are designed to enhance their lives in meaningful ways.

Here are some practical examples:

1. A small business owner creating eco-friendly products who joins online sustainability groups. By actively participating and showcasing their dedication to environmental conservation, they attract customers who prioritize sustainability.
2. An entrepreneur offering career coaching services might engage in professional networking groups, providing invaluable advice and aligning their brand with the aspirations of ambitious professionals.

3. A fitness coach can join local fitness communities, sharing their expertise and resonating with members who value health and wellness.

4. A clothing brand advocating for body positivity can connect with advocacy groups, empowering their clientele and fostering a supportive brand image.

Lastly, don't limit yourself to familiar territory. Broaden your outreach by networking with individuals from diverse industries or partnering with organizations that share your values. Conducting market research through focus groups or surveys can reveal deeper insights into your target audience's beliefs, which you can then integrate into your brand strategy.

Seeing this strategy come to life can be incredibly inspiring. Let's look at some global brands to see how they align their brand values with potential customers:

Patagonia - This outdoor apparel brand has successfully resonated with its ideal clients by promoting environmental sustainability and ethical sourcing. Their customer base, which holds strong beliefs in environmentalism and conscious consumerism, finds a kindred spirit in Patagonia. This alignment has not only strengthened their trust in the brand but also deepened their loyalty.

Nike's iconic "Just Do It" - This slogan aligns seamlessly with their ideal client's belief in perseverance and determination, striking a chord with athletes and sports enthusiasts around the globe. By sticking to a message that echoes the values of its core audience, Nike has built a brand that embodies the spirit of athleticism and resilience.

Dove's Real Beauty Campaign - By challenging traditional beauty standards, Dove aligns with its customers' beliefs in inclusivity and body positivity. This campaign not only created a powerful emotional connection with their audience but also positioned Dove as a champion of a progressive and inclusive vision of beauty, further solidifying customer loyalty.

Airbnb's "Belong Anywhere" messaging - It resonates profoundly with their ideal clients' beliefs in cultural diversity and the love for travel. This messaging has cultivated a sense of global community and belonging among Airbnb users, establishing a strong emotional bond and brand loyalty.

By developing an intentional branding voice that aligns with your ideal client's beliefs, you safeguard yourself from making this costly mistake. This approach not only attracts a loyal customer base outside of your current reach, but it also ensures that your brand remains relevant and connected in a meaningful way to those it aims to serve. It is this alignment that transforms casual customers into impassioned brand advocates.

Helpful Resources

There are several tools that entrepreneurs and small business owners can use to prevent the mistake of not aligning their brand values and messaging with their ideal client's beliefs.

- **The Ideal Client Map online companion members area** – Chapter 13
  - ➢ Access Resources here: https://resources.theidealclientmap.com

- Social media listening tools like Mention: These tools allow you to monitor conversations and trends in your industry, helping you stay in tune with your ideal client's beliefs and values.

- To truly understand your ideal client's values and beliefs, using a combination of qualitative and quantitative research methods is key. Start with surveys and questionnaires using platforms like SurveyMonkey or Google Forms. Craft questions that dig deep into their values, such as what qualities they appreciate in a brand or product and what factors influence their purchasing decisions.

- Customer feedback and reviews on platforms like Trustpilot or Yelp are treasure troves of information. They can highlight what your clients appreciate or criticize about your offers and provide invaluable insights into their ethical considerations and beliefs.

Take the time to explore these tools or similar ones, as they can help you develop a branding voice that truly resonates with your ideal client in the future. By understanding their beliefs and values, you can ensure that your brand messaging aligns with their mindset, ultimately leading to stronger connections and increased business success.

Anza's #1 Piece of Advice
If you have fallen out of alignment with your brand values with your ideal client's beliefs: Collaborate and network. By connecting with other small business owners outside of your immediate circle, you can gain valuable perspectives and insights that can help you align your brand values with your ideal client's beliefs. Networking allows you to step outside your comfort zone and engage with a diverse range of voices and experiences. This exposure can provide you with fresh ideas and innovative approaches that resonate with your target audience. To take it a step further, by engaging with a broader community, you are not only expanding your professional network but also creating opportunities for partnerships that can amplify your brand messaging and values.

When you align your brand values with your ideal client's beliefs, you create a strong connection that goes beyond just providing a product or service. It shows that you share common values and are invested in the same things. This creates a deeper level of trust and loyalty from your clients and helps to differentiate your brand from others in the market.

Check out these examples:

1. A yoga coach partnering with a wellness brand to create a transformative online yoga program.

2. A wellness coach collaborating with a luxury retreat to curate an exclusive wellness experience.

3. An executive coach teaming up with a high-profile CEO to lead a dynamic seminar on transformative leadership or strategic decision-making.

It's important to remember that your ideal client is not just a customer but a person who shares the same values and beliefs as your brand. By aligning your brand values with theirs, you are building a long-term relationship that goes beyond just a transaction. This connection is crucial for building a loyal customer base and attracting new clients who resonate with your brand's values. Now that you understand the importance of aligning your brand values with your ideal client's beliefs, take action on what you've learned in this chapter.

What We Covered

- Connect with potential clients outside of your immediate circle
- Research and understand the values and beliefs of your target audience
- Engage in conversations, surveys, and social listening to gain insight
- Use information to ensure brand values and messaging resonate with ideal clients
- Proactively align your brand with beliefs of ideal clients to avoid future mistakes

What Did You Learn?

1. Why is it crucial for your brand's core values to align with your client's beliefs?
   A. It makes marketing efforts more challenging
   B. It hinders your ability to achieve sustainable growth and long-term success
   C. It has no impact on building trust and loyalty with your clients
   D. It doesn't affect your ability to attract and retain customers

2. Kelcey's broad approach to addressing different types of life transitions was effective. - True /False

3. Why do entrepreneurs and small business owners struggle to align their brand values with their ideal client's beliefs?
   A. Lack of clarity and understanding of who their ideal client truly is
   B. Gaps in resources or knowledge needed to research and understand client beliefs
   C. Prioritizing personal values over those of their ideal clients
   D. All of the above

4. Failing to engage with a broader audience means you're missing a critical chance to align your brand values with the ______________ and needs of your ideal clients beyond your current reach.

5. What is a foundational step towards building a brand that attracts, retains, and delights its clientele?
   A. Investing in generic marketing tactics
   B. Prioritizing personal values over those of your ideal clients
   C. Understanding and aligning with your ideal client's beliefs
   D. Having a lack of clarity and understanding of who your ideal client truly is

6. To thrive, you must engage actively with future clients, demonstrate ______________, and align meaningfully with their beliefs and expectations.

7. Kelcey's strategic approach involved evaluating her products and services, scrutinizing the language she used, and planning effective communication with her target audience. - True / False

Find the Answer Key in the Online Companion Members Area

We've seen the critical importance of aligning your brand values with the beliefs of your ideal clients in this chapter. When your brand doesn't resonate with the core beliefs of your target audience, it makes the crucial tasks of building trust and loyalty considerably more challenging. Remember, true success is measured not just by the number of sales you achieve, but by the depth of relationships you cultivate. Building these meaningful connections is what turns simple transactions into lifelong partnerships, ultimately enriching both your brand and its community.

Conclusion

Congratulations! You've just finished reading "**The Ideal Client Map**: The Entrepreneur's Guide to Creating a Clear Branding Strategy and Actionable Marketing Plan So You Can Reach More Qualified Leads." You are now equipped with the knowledge and tools to take your business to the next level.

We hope you found this book to be a valuable resource in understanding the importance of identifying your ideal client and creating a clear branding strategy and actionable marketing plan. As an entrepreneur or small business owner, your time is precious, and it's essential that you focus on activities that will have the greatest impact on your business development. The Ideal Client Map provides a framework to help you do just that.

Now that you've gained a deeper understanding of the mistakes to avoid and practical advice, tips, and tricks to master this important aspect of your business, it's time to take action. Implement the strategies and techniques you've learned to reach more qualified leads and make a bigger impact in your industry.

To further support you on this journey, We encourage you to navigate your web browser to https://mapyouridealclient.com. There, you'll find the actual Ideal Client Map and training to quickly start using it. This resource will help guide you in applying the concepts from the book to your own business, ensuring that you see real results from your efforts.

Remember, success doesn't happen by chance. It takes intentional action and the right strategies to reach your goals. By utilizing the Ideal Client Map and the training provided, you'll be well on your way to attracting the clients and customers who are the best fit for your business.

Thank you for taking the time to invest in your business development by reading "The Ideal Client Map." We're confident that with the knowledge and tools you've gained, you will see a positive impact on your business. Here's to your continued success!

The Next Logical Step

Attention Entrepreneur and Small Business Owner:

Are you tired of struggling to find and attract your ideal clients? Do you feel like you're always chasing after the wrong leads and wasting your time and resources?

Introducing The Ideal Client Map Training, the ultimate solution to help you identify, target, and attract your perfect customers. This comprehensive training program is designed specifically for entrepreneurs and small business owners who are serious about growing their businesses and expanding their client base.

In this training, you will learn how to:

- Define your ideal client profile
- Craft compelling messaging to attract your ideal clients
- Develop a strategic map to reach and connect with your ideal clients

Say goodbye to wasted hours and missed opportunities, and start seeing real results in your business development efforts. Don't miss out on this exclusive training opportunity.

Grab The Ideal Client Map Training at http://mapyouridealclient.com and take the first step towards business success.

Glossary

Avatar: A visual or written representation of a person, often used in marketing to depict a target audience. Relevant to entrepreneurs and small business owners as it helps them create a clear picture of their ideal client and effectively tailor their marketing efforts.

Brand: The unique identity and image of a business or product. Relevant to entrepreneurs and small business owners as it emphasizes the importance of understanding their ideal client to develop a brand that resonates with their target audience.

Demographics: Statistical data that describes the characteristics of a specific population, such as age, gender, income, and education. Relevant to entrepreneurs and small business owners as it helps them understand the basic traits of their ideal client and tailor their marketing efforts accordingly.

Development: The process of creating, improving, or enhancing something over time. Relevant to entrepreneurs and small business owners as it highlights the importance of continually refining their understanding of their ideal client and adapting their products or services to meet their needs effectively.

Ideal Client: The specific type of customer or client that is the best fit for your business. Identifying and focusing on your ideal client allows for more effective marketing and higher customer satisfaction. Relevant to entrepreneurs and small business owners as it helps them narrow down their target market and create a stronger connection with their audience.

Ideal Client Avatar (ICA): A detailed and fictional representation of your ideal client. It includes demographic information, interests, behavior, and pain points. Relevant to entrepreneurs and small business owners as it helps them understand their target audience and tailor their products or services to meet their needs.

Marketing Plan: A strategic document that outlines a company's advertising and marketing efforts. Relevant to entrepreneurs and small business owners as it requires a deep understanding of their ideal client to create targeted and effective marketing strategies.

Marketing Research: The process of gathering, analyzing, and interpreting information about a market, including its ideal clients. Relevant to entrepreneurs and small business owners as it provides valuable insights into their ideal client's needs, preferences, and behaviors.

Persona: A detailed description of an ideal client or customer, including their characteristics, behaviors, and preferences. Relevant to entrepreneurs and small business owners as it helps them understand their target audience at a deeper level and create more personalized marketing strategies.

Psychographics: The study and classification of people according to their attitudes, values, beliefs, and lifestyles. Relevant to entrepreneurs and small business owners as it helps them understand the deeper motivations and behaviors of their ideal client, allowing for more targeted marketing strategies.

The Ideal Client Map (TICM): A visual representation that outlines the characteristics, behaviors, and preferences of the ideal client. Relevant to entrepreneurs and small business owners as it provides a structured way to document and understand their ideal client, helping them develop more effective marketing strategies.

Printed in the USA
CPSIA information can be obtained
at www.ICGtesting.com
LVHW011936211024
794443LV00013B/130

9 798218 524456